THE MORAL AND POLITICAL TRADITION OF ROME

ASPECTS OF GREEK AND ROMAN LIFE

General Editor: the late Professor H. H. Scullard

THE MORAL AND POLITICAL TRADITION OF ROME

Donald Earl

T&H

THAMES AND HUDSON

First published in paperback in 1984

Printed and bound in the U.S.A.

CONTENTS

For

E. M. F.

PREFACE

'THE PURPOSE OF THE ARISTOCRAT is to lead, therefore his functions are military and political'. Thus Miss Nancy Mitford on the English aristocracy. Her words could with equal justice be applied to the nobility of the Roman Republic and to the aristocracy which succeeded it. Indeed, whenever and wherever throughout the history of western civilization an aristocracy has emerged it has thus conceived its function. Sharing a common conception of their function, aristocracies tend to define their ideals in similar terms. The ideal of the Roman nobility is, in itself, neither remarkable nor unique. What makes it remarkable is the powerful influence it exerted far beyond the class to which it originally belonged. For from being the ideal of the nobility of the Republic it became the standard of the governing class of the Empire. From it developed the nearest approach the Romans made to a philosophy of history and a theory of historical processes. Moulded into a tradition of quite extraordinary longevity and vitality, it formed to the end of the Roman empire in the west the most potent influence on all educated Romans. It became, in a word, *the* Roman tradition.

The development of this tradition is the subject of the present book. When I received the invitation to contribute this volume to the series of handbooks on Greek and Roman Life, I had for some time been engaged in collecting material for a full history of the concept of *Virtus Romana* from the second century BC, when adequate information first becomes available, to St Augustine. Enough material had already been collected to convince me that the resulting book would be so inhumanly vast as to be probably unpublishable and certainly unreadable even by heroes. In writing the present book I was first tempted simply to boil down what I had already collected to the volume indicated by the publishers. I rapidly realized, however, that what would result would be a stew turgid with names and references but extremely thin in nutritious content. I therefore decided instead to concentrate my attention on the moral and political tradition of Rome as interpreted by major authors at important stages of Roman history. The result, though rather more impressionistic than my first plan, will, I hope, prove more approachable and informative and does not, I believe, distort the essential process of development of the tradition.

A further difficulty was that I have already published fairly extensively on the subject matter of the first two chapters. Strict academic etiquette would, I suppose, have obliged me briefly to mention these earlier discussions and then rapidly to proceed to new material. When, however, I considered that this series was directed not only nor primarily to the professional scholar, who will, in any case, find little that is new anywhere in this book, and that such exclusion would lead to eccentricity of treatment in the earlier chapters and leave those which followed without a proper foundation for understanding the later development of the tradition, I decided to consult the convenience of the reader by including in some detail, though in different form, the substance of my previous examinations of Roman *virtus* in the second and first centuries BC.

In return I must ask an indulgence from those readers who are not professional students of Roman civilization and who may even know no Latin, if there be any such who take up this book. My subject is something peculiarly Roman, which existed only within the culture which gave it birth and sustained it. Consequently I have preferred to retain the Latin names for the key concepts. These names, indeed, are untranslatable. That *nobilitas* is not 'nobility', that *fides* is not 'honesty', that *virtus* is not 'virtue', there precisely resides the subject of and reason for this book.

This book was written during my tenure of a visting professorship in the Department of Classical Languages of Northwestern University. I wish to express my sincere gratitude to the administration and faculty at Northwestern for their kindness and hospitality to me and my family, and especially to Professor Carl A. Roebuck, chairman of the Classics Department, and to Professor Anthony J. Podlecki, who read this book in manuscript. I also wish to thank the many audiences in various parts of the United States who listened to various parts of this book in various stages of development and not least the members of those audiences who disagreed with my views. My thanks are also due to Dr A. H. McDonald, Mr A. G. Woodhead and Professor Ernst Badian for suggestions and corrections.

Evanston, Illinois, D. C. E.
1 April 1966

CHAPTER I

MORALITY AND POLITICS

'A most stern reviler and judge of other men's luxury'.[1]

MACROBIUS' ASSESSMENT of the historian Sallust may not unfairly be taken as the epitome of the popular view of the Roman character as a whole. On the one side stand grave and reverend senators, unbendingly devoted to the public service and administering a world empire with severe and impartial justice. On the other recline abandoned voluptuaries, given over to orgiastic corruption and the more recondite delights of the most exquisite depravity. The former picture is, perhaps, less common today than in the days of Britain's imperial mission; the latter has been assiduously fostered by the arts of the cinema and of the popular novel. Both are caricatures. Yet a caricature is merely the grotesque exaggeration of lineaments existing in the original. For both pictures the Romans themselves are ultimately responsible. It is not necessary to read very far into their literature to discover that they were much obsessed by morality.

It is necessary, however, to be clear whom we mean by 'the Romans' in this or any other context. Essentially the history of the Roman Republic is the history of the small, literate upper class at Rome. The great monuments of Latin history and oratory, philosophy and poetry were, for the most part, produced by members of this upper class themselves or under their patronage. Consequently in the field of thought and ideas it is of this class only that we can speak in detail. An occasional literary reference, an isolated and unusually communicative tombstone may give us a glimpse of the aims and aspirations of the lower orders which comprised the vast majority of the population of Rome and of her Empire. But these remain disconnected data. The majority has disappeared silently and their thoughts must remain forever obscure. The minority alone remains, vociferously articulate, for posterity.

Further, it is not only that within a particular field our study must centre on the upper class; our choice of fields of study is dictated by this class. Since the sources from which we must work were produced by the upper class, the history we can write must mirror the pretensions and interests of this class. Since the concern of the upper class at Rome was almost exclusively with politics and statecraft, military and political history is the only history we have enough information to write, in the sense of being able to trace processes and developments in some detail over extended periods of time. Just as within the history of thought and ideas the vast majority of Romans have left us only brief and disjointed glimpses, so for whole fields of historical study, such as, for instance, sociology or economics, we have only isolated and tantalizing scraps of information. These often enigmatic data can, are and must be put together in an attempt to form a picture, but it remains impossible to write a proper demographic or economic history of Republican Rome in anything like the way we can write a military or political history.

The chief business of the upper class in Republican Rome was with politics and of this it maintained almost exclusive control. The earlier centuries of the Republic were marked externally by continuous warfare with Rome's nearer neighbours and the beginning of the slow extension of Roman power over the Italian peninsula. Internally these centuries saw the struggle of the Plebeian majority for political, social and economic equality with the Patrician minority. The purely political ambitions, it may be supposed, were reserved to the wealthier leaders of the Plebeian agitation. At all events, with the closing of the Struggle of the Orders the leading Plebeian families united with the Patricians, now in continuous and rapid decline, to form a new aristocracy which was distinguished by the term *nobilitas*.[2] It was a *political* aristocracy, defined precisely by the holding of political power and political office. In its strictest definition, in the last century BC, *nobilitas* was restricted to those families of which one member at least, either in the past or in the present, had attained the consulship. Earlier, in the second century, the qualification for nobility may have been wider, but the basis was still the holding of public office. The first man in a family to reach, in the second century, any of the curule magistracies (that is, under normal conditions, the consulship, praetorship and curule aedileship), in the first, the consulship became *nobilis* himself and as *auctor* or *princeps nobilitatis* ennobled his family forever. Of such new men the aristocracy was more tolerant than certain statements of political polemic or personal vainglory might suggest.[3] The Roman nobility was always of great vitality and ever in search of talent. Its attitude was one not of rigorous exclusion of outsiders but of carefully controlled inclusion. The lists of consuls provide proof. The consulate conferred supreme power and in the age of Cicero formed the title to *nobilitas*. Yet in the period from 200 BC to Marius' candidature for his first consulship no fewer than twenty-nine consuls seem to come from new families. Exactly how many of these families were new in the sense of being not merely non-consular but non-senatorial is difficult to determine: perhaps nearly half the total. Similarly between 100 and 64 BC eleven new men of non-consular family held the consulship. These are minimum figures, based on the appearance of new names. That between one in six and one in eight of the consuls in the century and a half that followed the defeat of Hannibal would come from new families is sufficient indication that the Roman aristocracy was not rigorously exclusive of all new men at all costs, not even from the highest office of state. On the contrary, the Roman oligarchy was in a state of continuous recruitment and regeneration. Many of the new men, promoted for personal talent or, more rarely, for the convenience of the nobility, remained isolated examples: their descendants, though sometimes to be detected in the lower ranks of the Senate, lapsed from eminence. But others founded powerful political families which took their places only little inferior to aristocratic houses of fabulous antiquity. The third and second centuries BC provide many examples: Sempronii, for instance, Mucii Scaevolae, Porcii Catones, Octavii, Calpurnii Pisones—the last proverbial in the late Republic and early Principate for antiquity of lineage.[4] The origin, standing and achievement of the new men were diverse. In the second century M. Porcius Cato rose from a non-senatorial family to become one of the leaders of the state and an instigator of public policy.[5] Cn. Octavius achieved the consulate of 165 after both he and his father had served the Republic well.[6] P. Rupilius, consul in 132, was the merest nonentity who owed everything to the patronage of the great Scipio Aemilianus.[7] Very few of the new men were honest sons of toil or boys fresh from the plough. They came, in the main, from the local aristocracies in the Roman townships in Italy. Men like Cato the Censor, Marius or Cicero were powerful nobles in their native towns, though their families counted for little at Rome. Throughout Italy the local aristocracies in the various towns, engrossing political power and social position, mirrored the senatorial nobility of Rome which, in turn, was always on the look-out for young men of talent and promise who might be introduced into the public life of the capital. By the middle of the first century BC the Roman nobility was an heterogeneous body. Families of extreme antiquity vied with others of much more recent origin. The most extreme and efficient faction of the oligarchy was led and animated by the younger M. Porcius Cato. His great-grandfather had been a farmer in the Sabine country, introduced to Rome by the Patrician L. Valerius Flaccus.

Yet such new men succeeded at Rome because they accepted the standards of the capital and, even more important, because they were admitted and promoted by members of the existing oligarchy. The real power lay with a core of twenty or fewer families who commanded armies, governed the provinces and by guiding the policy of the Senate shaped the destiny of Rome and of the western world. With the passage of the generations the composition of this oligarchy changed slowly. Some families slipped from power, others rose to take their place. But in any age of the Roman Republic of this central, controlling oligarchy is starkly documented in the lists of magistrates and priests.

The power of this oligarchy, indeed of the governing class as a whole, rested not on any legal or constitutional enactment but merely on its ability to control the votes of the Roman People. Before the law the *nobilis*, with the exception of the Patricians who retained from an earlier age a few, largely decorative, privileges, was in no different position from any other member of the Roman citizen body. The methods by which the nobility maintained its control over the Roman People, especially over the electoral assemblies which generation after generation returned members of the same few families to office and power, are not entirely clear. But the basis of the political power of the nobility may be found in the institution of 'clientship', *clientela*, by which the lower orders of society were closely bound to the various noble families in a relation of mutual benefit.[8] A noble patron would help and protect his client in various ways and thus create reciprocal obligations, the chief of which was for the client to support his patron in his political career. It was through this complex nexus of personal and extra-constitutional relationships that the nobility controlled not only the people of Rome but the whole of Italy, by its ties of *clientela* with the leading men in both Roman and Allied communities. In the second century BC and later the concept was exported oversea and provincial *clientelae* were used first for display and to enhance the prestige of the individual noble and then for direct and menacing influence on the political struggles of the capital.[9] It is clear that an informal arrangement of this kind could have succeeded only with the acquiescence of the Roman People at large. The vast majority of Roman citizens had not fallen into the modern error of supposing that political systems were important to anyone but the politicians. They looked on government as a service, the chief purpose of which was to provide internal stability and freedom from interference so that the important business of life could proceed unhindered. So long as the individual noble protected his client, so long as the government assured stability for the citizens, the governed and the clients were content to leave politics to the politicians. It is remarkable that at no time, not even when the Republic was perishing amid civil war, can anything like a sustained popular movement be detected among the Roman People. Discontents existed in all ages, but they influenced political life only when used by the politicians for their own ends. The ordinary Roman asked only for stability and freedom from interference, and a dictatorship of the type established by Caesar, if accompanied by these minimum benefits, suited him as well as any amount of Republican liberty.[10] It was because the Republican nobility failed ultimately to provide these benefits that it failed to interest the ordinary Roman in its survival. It was the great strength of the emperor Augustus that he at last restored conditions in which normal life was again possible. Men from the political class might sneer at 'peace and a prince', but if monarchy was the price of internal stability, it was a price that the Roman People paid and paid gladly.

Assured of the uninterrupted enjoyment of political power, the Republican nobility was consumed within itself by a fierce and incessant competition for position. Within the nobility the basic political unit was the family group. Noble families formed alliances with each other the better to further the ambitions of their members—or to attack their enemies. Such factions, with the ties of mutual interest frequently cemented by those of marriage, were usually *ad hoc* arrangements. But in the course of time certain lines of alliance became traditional, though always liable to modification by reason of personal ambition, antipathy or opportunism, or even the interest of the state. Very occasionally the competing factions of the nobility would close ranks to face some quite exceptional crisis. But to the Roman noble the pursuit of power and glory, position and prestige was paramount. It was this that he equated with the Roman Republic.[11]

It will be apparent that the politics of the Roman Republic were social and personal. Nothing remotely like a modern political party existed and any attempt to force Roman politics into an alien mould constructed on the pattern of a modern two party state can only obscure and mislead. The temptation is strong to impose a familiar order on the, to us, unfamiliar disorder of Roman political life by seeing it, often unconsciously, in terms of a two-party system: Optimates and Populares, Senate and Businessmen, Senate and People, Caesarians and Pompeians. Such abstractions, though they may find apparent support in political propaganda, have no place in the realities of Roman politics. Nor is there much evidence that the average noble politician subscribed to a consistent political philosophy in the sense that a modern man might, for instance, term himself a 'liberal' or 'radical', though a member of no political party, and thus lay claim to a set of attitudes and principles which he would consistently follow in his judgement of public affairs. At Rome politics dealt with individuals and factions, not political parties, with personalities, not programmes.

Since politics at Rome were personal and social, the language of politics mirrors this condition. All Romans saw political issues in personal and social terms, that is, in terms of morality. Again the categories are ours, not theirs. The Romans did not distinguish morality sharply from politics or economics but looked at affairs from a point of view which may be termed 'social', reflecting the personal and social nature of political life itself. Thus, where we would see the working of the processes of economic change and sociological and political adjustment, they saw—or appear to us to have seen—only ethical issues. A clear example is the Roman tradition in the second century BC. To us this period appears as one of great economic, social and political change with the influx into Rome and Italy of vast wealth from the booty of the Eastern wars, an increase in the standard of living accompanied by massive inflation, the failure of much of southern Italy to recover from the Hannibalic devastation, a gradual but continuing depopulation of the Italian countryside and a concomitant increase in the unemployed proletariate in Rome, the acquisition by Rome of a world empire and the failure of the senatorial nobility to realize its implications. But when we turn to the Roman writers on the period we find little of these complicated and interacting factors. Instead we meet a firm insistence that by the middle of the second century BC Rome had undergone a moral crisis from which she never recovered. Thus the annalistic tradition presented by Livy and drawing on contemporary material ascribed the crisis to the return of Manlius Vulso's army from Asia in 187 BC.[12] The booty, which included costly and elaborate furniture, and luxurious habits, including a respect for fine cooking, acquired in the East formed the 'beginning of foreign luxury' and the 'seeds of the future luxury' which was later to destroy the Roman way of life. The Greek historian of Rome, Polybius, while of the opinion that from 200 BC onwards there was some decline in moral standards, placed the crisis in the years after Rome had achieved universal domination, that is after 168 BC.[13] Writing of the desire of the young Scipio Aemilianus to lead a virtuous life, Polybius contrasted it with the general deterioration of morals which included homosexuality, whoring and elaborate and costly banquets. Such debauchery, we are told, arose from contact with Greek dissoluteness during the war with Perseus and, after his defeat, burst into flame.[14] The annalist L. Calpurnius Piso, although he seems to have given an account of the return of Manlius Vulso's army similar to that of Livy, appears to have held that the year 154 BC marked the turning point in moral decline, for it was then that 'chastity was overthrown'.[15] Polybius again says that the chief motive of the Senate in declaring war on Dalmatia was to restore the moral fibre of the Romans who had become enervated by long peace, it being now the twelfth year since the war with Perseus.[16] The great debate on the destruction of Carthage has left its mark on the tradition as being largely concerned with moral issues. Scipio Nasica urged the preservation of Rome's great enemy on the ground that the existence of an external threat was essential to the maintenance of moral standards at Rome.[17] The historian Sallust accepted Nasica's case and his choice of the destruction of Carthage as the moment of the great moral crisis set a fashion. His words may stand as an epitome of the Roman attitude:

'Thus at home and abroad high moral standards were cultivated. There was the greatest harmony, the least avarice. Right and good influenced the men of those days more by nature than by laws. . . . But when the state had grown great through toil and justice, when great kings had been overcome in war, when wild tribes and huge nations had been subdued by force, when Carthage, the rival of Roman power, had been utterly destroyed and everything lay open to Rome on land and sea, then fortune began to rage and throw everything into confusion. To men who had easily borne toil, danger, doubt and difficulty, peace and riches, which would have been desirable at other times, became a burden and a misery. There grew up first the lust for money, then the lust for power. These were, so to speak, the raw materials of all the other evils. For avarice overturned good faith, uprightness and the other moral qualities. In their place it taught arrogance, cruelty, neglect of the gods and the belief that everything could be bought and sold. Ambition induced many men to become false, to have one thing locked in their breasts, another ready on their tongues, to judge friendships and enmities not on the basis of fact but on that of advantage, to have a fair face rather than a fair mind.'[18] With the return of Sulla's army from Asia, according to Sallust, a further stage of degeneration was reached which resulted in the complete overthrow of all moral standards.[19] The thought and formulation are alike thoroughly traditional. The passage also illustrates the impotence of the Roman mind once it moved outside the familiar moral concepts. The best that Sallust could do to explain why the destruction of Carthage brought such dire results was a feeble invocation of fortune.

Nor was it merely the historian, attempting to explain historical processes over a period of time, who represented political and economic issues and crises as moral ones. Cato the Censor and Scipio Aemilianus, treating in their speeches the problems of the second century as contemporaries, adopted the same standpoint as the later historians. And all Roman political invective shows an obsession with morality. It became obligatory to accuse your political opponent of all the more recondite forms of private vice. The quasi-technical vocabulary of politics proper, which was based to a great extent on a terminology originally expressing ethical concepts, behaved similarly. But to take an already existing moral term and to redefine it for a political purpose was not to destroy the old but to add a new dimension to what already existed. Thus the word *boni*, 'good men', not merely denoted a specific group of people in politics but at the same time asserted their general moral worth and their right to power because of this worth. Again, a specifically political concept of *virtus* can, as we shall see, be isolated. But in thus isolating it, we in a sense do violence to the Latin usage. When a Roman politician, whether *nobilis* or *novus*, asserted the rights of *virtus*, he laid claim to the whole complex of moral ideas for which the word stood. All this makes the vocabulary of Roman politics singularly difficult to handle. Words are anything but fixed. Meanings will not stay in place but slip and slide into each other. For the ancient publicist and propagandist this was a great advantage. Hence the continuous process of development, re-affirmation and re-definition which makes the Roman political language a truly living one down to the end of the Republic and beyond. But to the modern enquirer striving to fix the exact reference, to distinguish the technical and precise from the imprecise and popular, the political particular from the moral general, the nature of the Roman political vocabulary causes great difficulty and the permanent Roman habit of apparently puritanical moralizing brings extreme exasperation. But the difficulty and exasperation are of our own making. Action, thought and expression form a unity. The Romans, on the whole, lacked either interest in or capacity for abstract political theorizing. To the Republican politician politics was a personal and social matter. He therefore thought and expressed his thought in personal and social terms, that is, in the language, above all, of morality.[20]

The Republican nobility expressed its ideal in the concept of *virtus*.[21] The word, like many others with which we shall have to deal, is not translatable. 'Manliness' is perhaps the nearest we we can get. Fundamentally it describes the peculiar nature and quality of the man, *vir*, as *senectus*, old age, describes the quality peculiar to the *senex*, old man, and *iuventus*, youth, that peculiar to the *iuvenis*, young man.[22] But, whereas youth and old age are defined largely by external and objective criteria, *virtus* is essentially a subjective concept. As one's notion of the particular end of man varies, so will one's definition of his proper activity and quality. Define the end of man as to achieve maximum material prosperity and *virtus* may consist in the more or less ruthless acquisition of money. Define it as the salvation of an immortal soul and *virtus* may consist in prayer, contemplation and withdrawal from the world. The Roman aristocrat was above all a political animal. Left, as we have seen, in the uninterrupted enjoyment of political power and position, he defined his ideal way of life as above all political. *Virtus*, for the Republican noble, consisted in the winning of personal pre-eminence and glory by the commission of great deeds in the service of the Roman state. It is with this concept, or rather complex of concepts that we shall be concerned. For from being the ideal of a narrow ruling class it became accepted as the tradition of Rome herself and through many transformations and redefinitions survived not only the class that had first given it birth but even the civilization and culture to which it first belonged.

We first meet this ideal, asserted rather than reasoned, for these are funerary inscriptions, on a series of laudatory epitaphs dating from the end of the third and the first half of the second centuries BC. What appears to be the earliest of the series, the epitaph of L. Cornelius Scipio, begins with a splendidly confident statement of aristocratic pre-eminence: 'This one man most Romans agree was the best of all good men.'[23] A. Atilius Calatinus went one better: it was not merely the Romans but 'most nations' who agreed that he was 'the leading man among the Roman People'.[24] Scipio's epitaph supports its opening assertion with a record of his civil offices, military successes and services to the gods. These three areas of activity, the government, the army and the state religion, comprised the whole of public life, the last no less and no differently from the other two. The official religion of Rome was entirely formalistic, directed to maintenance of peace with the gods who often seem to have been regarded as a foreign power in treaty relations with the Roman state. Religious matters affecting the state directly were usually left to the civil magistrates who could consult the sacerdotal experts or not as they wished. In fact, so far from priestly office being a bar to political office, they normally went hand in hand and the religious colleges were composed of statesmen.[25] The state religion was merely one aspect of the government of the Republic and religious office, quite apart from any actual power it conferred, was regarded as enhancing a politician's dignity and prestige in much the same way as the more important civil magistracies. Because religion was not divorced from civil government, but was considered rather as essentially the same activity viewed from a different standpoint, religious office frequently did invest the holder with considerable power which he could use or misuse for political ends.[26] The abuse of such power in the last century of the Republic is notorious and there is some evidence to suggest that even earlier the perversion of religious means for political ends was not entirely unknown. Certainly the number of times a religious decision advanced the career of Q. Fabius Maximus is suspicious.[27] But such perversion of religious power was probably not yet widespread. Polybius, writing about the middle of the second century BC, was able to praise the honesty and incorruptibility of the Roman nobility in matters of religion.[28]

The epitaph of L. Cornelius Scipio Barbatus, the father of the Scipio whose epitaph has just been mentioned, is in one respect more explicit.[29] Instead of an indefinite assertion of pre-eminence, Barbatus is characterized as a 'brave and wise man', as possessing, that is, the two most important qualities for a leader of armies and for a magistrate and counsellor.[30] More explicit still are two epitaphs in honour of men who died too young to hold public office. One makes clear the whole aristocratic ideal of a successful life: 'Office, fame, *virtus*, glory and natural talent.' Man's proper ambition is for glory gained by great deeds and the standard by which success is judged is the glory attained by his ancestors.[31] The other inscription warns us 'do not look for his offices since none were entrusted to him'.[32] As Professor R. E. Smith has put it, 'we see the constancy of the ideal, consisting still in public honours and public office, to the extent that even when the dead man took no part in public life, the only comment is on what he would have done had he lived longer'.[33] But the subject of the epitaph is also described as 'never conquered in *virtus*'. While it was usual to display and enhance one's *virtus* by one's deeds in public life, as Barbatus and his son are recorded to have done, it was also possible to show the potentiality in earlier life in private affairs and the activities proper to young men before they entered the career of public office. When a man had advanced in this career, the aristocratic tradition, with its concentration on the service of the state, found it unnecessary to record personal qualities or achievements outside this all-important area. The service of the state required private virtues, but in their public application. To a purely private cultivation of personal virtue the Roman tradition was always hostile. The tradition prescribed the service of the state as the only fit field of activity. The proper service of the state demanded private goodness, but such goodness without public achievement was of no account. The tradition was, as we shall see, very persistent. It forms the basis of Tacitus' attacks on the Stoic opposition under the Empire. And it was not confined to a condemnation of philosophic detachment from the mundane. All social standing and position were obtainable only through the service of the Republic. In this tradition terms denoting laziness, such as *ignavia* and *inertia*, have a sharp and definite connotation: refusal to play a part in politics. The attacks on the *piscinarii*, those men who in the age of Cicero retired to their country estates and the opulent contemplation of their fishponds, were directed not mainly at their wealth and luxury, which they often shared with those who attacked them, but at their non-involvement in public affairs. Sallust gave up a public career to write history. In his handling of his retirement in the prologues to his monographs on Catiline's conspiracy and the war with Jugurtha he is palpably on the defensive.[34] While hunting and agriculture were honourable enough pastimes to a man's main business, they ought not to engross the whole of his attention. It was for slaves to devote themselves utterly to such things. Nor, even, should intellectual pursuits like historiography take up a gentleman's whole time. A senator wrote history for pleasure or political profit; but he wrote in the intervals of a vigorous public career. It was not fit for a public man completely to withdraw from public life to devote himself to the writing of history at an age when office was still attainable. Sallust, even after the murder of Caesar, felt strongly the obligation to justify both his retirement and its occupation. He argued that history is, in fact, a form of public service: it excites men to the pursuit of political glory in the same way as do the busts of the ancestors in the atria of the great noble families.

The earliest expression of the aristocratic ideal is well summarized in the eulogy that Q. Metellus delivered at the funeral of his father, L. Caecilius Metellus, who died in 221 BC.[35] According to Pliny, Quintus left a written record of his father's life-long desire to be a warrior of the first rank, the best orator, the bravest general, to manage the greatest affairs on his own responsibility, to enjoy the greatest honour, to possess the highest wisdom, to be considered the most eminent senator, to acquire great wealth by honourable means, to leave many children and to be the most famous man in the state. The aim is the same as that expressed in the Scipionic epitaphs: to serve the Republic as warrior and general, orator and senator; to achieve by the commission of great deeds in this service a position of pre-eminence, emphasized here by the repeated superlatives; to be a man both brave and wise; to gain great honour through public office; to ensure the continuance of the family so that posterity might emulate and surpass the glory attained by its ancestors.[36]

The ideal thus sketched in these early monuments, the writers of the second century BC reflect and expand. Thus it would be difficult to find a clearer expression of devotion to the state than the prayer which Ennius put into the mouth of Decius Mus at the battle of Asculum: 'Gods, hear this briefly as steadfastly and with full deliberation I lay down my life for the Roman People fighting in battle'; or the sentence from a speech before the battle of Magnesia: 'Now is that day when the greatest glory shows herself to us whether we live or die.' Similarly the intimate connection between the state and the glory of the individual aristocrat is revealed in the famous fragment on Q. Fabius Maximus: 'One man by delaying restored the state to us. He refused to put rumour before our safety. Therefore, even now long afterwards the glory of the man shines forth with even greater radiance.'[37] Again, the way of life of the Roman aristocrat in time of peace is summed up in the character sketch of Servilius who spent the great part of the day exhausting himself in the management of the highest affairs of state by giving counsel in the forum and senate-house and who chose as his intimate friend another who would never commit an evil deed either through carelessness or malice, who was learned and faithful, charming and eloquent, satisfied with his lot, happy and shrewd, who said the right thing at the right time, was accessible and obliging, a man of few words who both retained many ancient ways and customs and also admitted the modern, who followed the customs of many men of old and the laws of gods and men, who was wise enough to speak what he had heard or to keep silent.[38]

The comic poet Plautus also had his uses for the aristocratic ideal. He employs it in two ways, for direct comment and for comic effect.[39] Not that the one excluded the other. The attribution to a slave engaged on a typical piece of servile deceit of high aristocratic pretensions could serve both as a good joke and as a sarcastic comment on the nobility. Thus he could use the broken mutterings of a breathless slave to mock the consecrated phraseology of the aristocratic tradition: 'Hurry, Pinacium, urge your feet, honourable words with deeds—now you have the power of winning glory, praise and honour—assist your needy mistress—the fine deeds of your ancestors.'[40] Again, when a slave says 'no one is powerful enough to withstand me on the road, not a strategus nor any tyrant nor an agoranomus nor a demarchus nor a comarchus nor anyone with so great glory, but he will fall, he will stand on his head in the road out of my path',[41] the point of the joke is obvious. Glory was for the Romans connected with public office, but with office of somewhat greater weight than these comic-opera positions. Such jokes form an exuberant strain of Plautine comedy.

On other occasions Plautus could be more thoughtful. His play *Trinummus* contains several passages that are best explained as alluding to the Roman political scene in the second decade of the second century BC when Cato was leading the attacks on the family and faction of the Cornelii Scipiones that culminated in the downfall of Scipio Africanus.[42] These passages refer to a clique of *boni* which was harming the state and are eloquent on the subject of the dominance in both public and private life of evil customs, *mores mali*. One of them is of especial interest for our enquiry. Lysiteles says to his friend Lesbonicus: 'Did your ancestors leave you this fame just so that you could lose by vice what they had won by *virtus*? So that you could become the champion of the honour of your ancestors, your father and grandfather made the path to the pursuit of office easy and smooth for you. But you have made it difficult by your own fault and idleness and stupid behaviour. You have preferred to rank love before *virtus*. Now do you think you can cover up your failings in this way? You can't. Get hold of *virtus* in your mind and cast out idleness from your heart. Help your friends in the forum, not your mistress in bed as you usually do.'[43] *Virtus* is here connected with the family, with honour and office, with the obligations of political association and alliance (*amicitia*), with the public life of the forum and with a certain standard of conduct. Now Polybius records a conversation between himself and the young Scipio Aemilianus in which the latter complained of the low esteem in which he was held: 'I am told that everyone thinks me idle and lazy and far removed from the true Roman character and energy because I do not choose to plead in the law-courts. They say that the family from which I come needs a champion not such as I am, but quite the opposite.'[44] The similarity between the speech in the comedy and the conversation recorded by the historian is remarkably close. There seems no possibility that Polybius copied Plautus. Rather the two passages, though from sources so disparate, belong in the same tradition. Both Scipio and Lesbonicus were accused of failing the ideal of the Roman aristocratic tradition in that they refused to play their proper part in public life and thus to enhance their families' glory. Although Scipio at the time of his complaint to Polybius was only eighteen years of age, the tradition demanded activity in an appropriate sector of public life. The activities prescribed for the apprenticeship of the young noble before he began the career of office proper were military service and pleading in the courts.

It will be apparent that the Roman aristocracy was possessed of extreme concern for the family and that the family consisted not merely of its living members but of the dead ancestors and the unborn posterity as well. Thus L. Caecilius Metellus, among his other great achievements, wished to leave many children. It was by the standard of his ancestors' glory that the value of a noble's deeds was judged. The noble who refused to take his proper place in public life disgraced not merely himself but his whole family and not only those members who were alive but his ancestors who had won glory and his posterity who would receive from him a diminished prestige. The whole procedure at the funeral of a Roman aristocrat was directed to commemorating the glory of the dead man and to perpetuating that of his ancestors. The funeral eulogy referred to the successes and great exploits not only of the deceased himself but of his great ancestors who were present in the form of wax busts, *imagines*, at the funeral.[45] The latest in the series of Scipionic epitaphs insists on the family in every line: 'I increased the merits of my race by my upright standards. I begot children. I followed the exploits of my father. I won the praise of my ancestors so that they rejoiced that I had been born to them. Honour ennobled my stock'.[46] This inscription dates from the end of the second century BC when the aristocracy had lost its earlier security and self-confidence and under various external and internal pressures had become increasingly self-conscious as to its position and prerogatives.[47] During the Spanish wars which began in the middle of the century the Roman armies, for the first time since Rome became the strongest power in the Mediterranean, suffered almost constant defeat and for the first time since the Senate had emerged as the dominant body in the Roman state, senatorial direction of policy was found wanting. It was not merely that the legions suffered defeat after defeat. The Senate as a body was quite unable to impose its authority on the individual commanders. The record of the Roman nobility in Spain at this time is one of incompetence, cruelty and treachery. In the Senate again and again military considerations and the interests of the Republic were subordinated to the ambition of individual politicians and factions. Rising agitation at Rome over the operation of the conscription levy led to the revival of the revolutionary powers inherent in the Plebeian tribunate. Tribunes not merely imprisoned consuls. In 139 and 137 they carried laws to introduce the secret ballot in the election of magistrates and in all trials before the People except those for treason.[48] These two measures cut deeply into the power of the nobility which rested in the last resort on its power to control the votes of the People. It was this that had prompted the careful organization of the lower orders of Roman society into *clientelae* by the various noble factions. It was this that caused the eagerness of each faction to enlarge its *clientela* in order to increase the voting power at its disposal and, as Rome's empire increased and the concept of *clientela* was extended from Rome to Italy and then to the provinces overseas, for prestige and propaganda. But if the vote was to be delivered in secret, then the noble patron would find it much less easy to be assured that his clients would continue to vote faithfully in his interest. They could no longer be called to account for the way they voted and would be much more open to seduction by their patron's political enemies. Then in 133 BC all the accumulated stresses burst forth and the tribunate of Tiberius Gracchus demonstrated conclusively the basic instability in the Senate's position.

'On the customs and men of old the Roman state is founded.' Cicero, quoting Ennius' great line, agreed that ancestral custom, *mos maiorum*, was essential to the Republic.[49] Indeed, he all but identified the two. Although Cicero was concerned with a much wider reinterpretation of the old idea, he and Ennius and all the others who praised the standards and traditions of the *maiores* were correct in their assessment. It was not merely, nor most importantly, that the Roman nobility shared the conservatism naturally inherent in all aristocracies. Something more fundamental and more concrete is implied. The maintenance of the power of the Roman nobility depended precisely on the conservation of the existing status. By the second century BC Roman politics, though a ceaseless struggle for position and power by the leading men, had achieved a fair degree of equilibrium, the preservation of which was a major concern of every faction in the noble oligarchy. Every individual and every faction aspired to a position of pre-eminence and predominance, which every other individual and faction conspired to prevent—and desired for themselves. Sometimes an individual or faction did attain a temporary predominance. Then the efforts of the other nobles were devoted to destroying this predominance in the shortest possible time. The fate of Scipio Africanus in the early years of the second century is the prime example. Just as the power of the senatorial oligarchy as a whole depended on its ability to control the voters at large, so within the oligarchy the power of each faction rested ultimately on its ability to control a specific section of the Roman People, its own clients. For by their votes it obtained the magistracies from which all prestige and position flowed. Hence the resistance to reform on the part of the Roman nobility. Given the existing political conditions, any reform of importance would have been likely to attract an increase of prestige and *clientela* to its sponsors and thus to upset the delicate political balance. It has been plausibly suggested that colonization in Italy came to an end in the second century BC precisely because the other noble factions were unwilling to allow a colony's sponsors to acquire control of such solid concentrations of Roman citizens. The protracted resistance of the Roman nobility to the enfranchisement of the Italian allies was founded not in blind selfishness or stupid conservatism but in sober political calculation. The sudden admission to the Roman citizenship of the mass of Italian allies appeared likely to destroy the Roman nobility's control both of Italy, by breaking the old ties of *clientela* with the allied states, and of the Roman People, by flooding the assemblies with new voters of doubtful allegiance.[50]

Further, it was not merely that the nobility had a vested interest in maintaining the present state. Its whole power and position was founded on custom and precedent. The organization of the People into *clientelae* and their acquiescence in the domination of political life by a small aristocratic oligarchy rested on no legal or constitutional foundation. Before the law and the constitution the noble had exactly the same status as the other members of the Roman community. His tangible privileges were few and unimportant. Similarly with the body through which the oligarchy worked. The Senate had emerged as the controlling and directing organ in the government of Rome. Yet technically it remained a private and unofficial body, the council of the magistrates, particularly of the consuls. Very few indeed of its powers and prerogatives were sanctioned by law. To the Roman nobility *mos maiorum*, custom and precedent, were the Republic in a very real sense. The Roman revolution began when a faction of the nobility, in prosecuting the incessant internal struggle of the oligarchy, ruthlessly exposed, in the tribunate of Ti. Gracchus, the lack of any solid constitutional foundation to the power of the Senate and the control of public life by the aristocracy.[51]

It was with good reason that the Roman noble appealed to custom and precedent. His whole way of life depended on them. In the ideology of the aristocracy, as we have seen, the standards and achievements of the ancestors formed the criteria by which those of the present generation were judged. In particular, the glory of the ancestors, *gloria maiorum*, was frequently invoked. *Gloria* is often found with *fama*, but the difference between the two concepts is important.[52] *Fama* means 'what is said' about a person or thing. Applied to a man it means 'reputation'. It is a neutral term. Anyone can acquire a reputation for anything, good or bad. Cicero, however, speaks of 'the good reputation of good men which alone can truly be termed *gloria*'. He defines *gloria* as 'praise given to right actions and the reputation for great merits in the service of the Republic which is approved not merely by the testimony of the multitude but by the witness of all the best men'.[53] Thus, although *fama* and *gloria* had common ground, the latter did not depend primarily on the opinion of the many but on that of the best men, of those who judge aright, of the *boni*, that is, of the political aristocracy. It was not a vague or a neutral concept. In this context it was specific and definite. *Gloria* was accorded by the political class for great and meritorious deeds in the service of the state. It is in this sense, though naturally not so explicitly as in the Ciceronian definitions, that we meet *gloria* in the *Annales* of Ennius and the plays of Plautus.[54] It was aristocratic and exclusive, awarded by the political class for political achievements.

But the mere doing of great deeds was not enough. The ideal of *virtus* also imposed a proper standard of conduct. This aspect, barely hinted at in the inscriptions, is made explicit by the poets. Thus Ennius ascribed to Pyrrhus a speech in reply to Fabricius who had come to ransom the Romans captured at Heraclea: 'I do not ask gold for myself nor will you pay a price to me. Not as peddlers of war but as warriors let us both decide the issues of life or death by iron, not gold. Let us make trial by *virtus* whether mistress Fortune wishes you or me to rule or whatever she may bring. At the same time receive this word: whose *virtus* in war Fortune has spared, their liberty have I also decided to spare. I give them, take them; and I give them with the good will of the mighty gods.'[55] Thus Pyrrhus called the Romans to conduct the war according to proper standards and not to stoop to sordid expedients. It was the Romans who were at fault. It was they who were trying to decide the issue by gold. It was they who wished to peddle, to buy and sell war, a biting phrase when set in the context of the aristocratic contempt for all forms of trade. For a man of senatorial rank all trade was held undignified and retail trade particularly contemptible.[56] The word *mercator*, merchant or trader, appears almost as a term of abuse.[57] Even a business man as cultured and acceptable as Cicero's friend Atticus was considered inferior to the meanest member of the Senate. It was a question of *dignitas*, the peculiar prestige which was held to be the attribute solely of senators and the importance of which to a senator was paramount.[58] This attitude in its extreme form derives to some extent from the greatly increased self-consciousness of the senatorial nobility in the revolutionary conditions of the first century BC, though even then, it must be pointed out, senators did not hesitate to enjoy the company of business men, to borrow their money and to marry their daughters. But the attitude was already well established by the beginning of the second century. It is reflected in the proem to Cato's handbook on agriculture and Plautus invariably treats the commercial classes with hostility and contempt.[59] Not that the aristocratic ideal excluded the acquisition of great wealth. It was one of the laudable ambitions of L. Caecilius Metellus to obtain a great fortune. But such wealth had to be acquired in a proper way, *bono modo*, which at this time probably meant in most cases by inheritance and investment in land. Further, wealth had to be used in the same way, for honourable ends. Ennius' contrast between iron, that is the sword, and gold recalls his words on M' Curius Dentatus 'whom no one could overcome by iron or gold'.[60] It was not disgraceful to be overcome by the sword. On the contrary, to die fighting for one's country was a pre-eminent way of winning *gloria*. The man who died *per virtutem* did not perish utterly since the glory he had thus won lived on after him.[61] To be overcome by money was a different matter. It was the Roman boast that 'it is not our pleasure to fight with money, reward or trickery'.[62] From this ideal Ennius pictured the Romans as having fallen. Pyrrhus was made to judge their conduct by their own standard. *Virtus* here stands not for courage simply but for the whole aristocratic ideal with its insistence on the winning of glory by the commission of great deeds in the service of the state according to certain standards of conduct. Similarly, when Flamininus 'watched the *virtus* of his army, waiting to see if it would grumble "What rest will there ever be from fighting or end to our hard labour" ', another fragment of the *Annales* lays down the principle 'it is not right that good men, who have brought forth deeds by exerting themselves in the labour of warfare, should grumble'.[63] Just as it was the duty of the good commander to preserve discipline, so it was the duty of the good soldier to observe the discipline imposed on him and to exert himself to great achievements. Both the noble commander and the common soldier were men of *virtus*, *boni*, in so far as they lived up to the standard.

For civil life Plautus provides evidence. In the prologue to the *Amphitruo* he contrasted *virtus* and *ambitio* in lines alluding to canvassing for a magistracy.[64] As the Roman People had won its great victories in war by *virtus*, so candidates for office and actors at dramatic contests should win theirs. *Ambitio*, although often connected with words denoting bribery, does not itself mean bribery simply. Rather it stands for the wrong method of reaching a good end, public office, by any form of electoral malpractice, whether bribery or the employment of electoral associations and cliques or the misuse of *clientela*. This last, the fundamental institution of Roman politics, is the subject of a long moralizing diatribe in Plautus' *Menaechmi*: 'How we most of all employ this stupid custom, harmful and excessive, and how all the best men particularly have this habit! They all wish to have many clients. Whether the clients are good or bad they don't enquire. The wealth of the clients is scrutinized rather than their good faith.'[65] Since the whole of Roman political life was organized on the basis of unofficial custom, the paramount quality was good faith, *fides*. It was the corner-stone of the patron-client relationship and ensured the stability of the factions formed among the members of the nobility. Cicero called it the foundation of justice and Caesar, conscious as ever of his Patrician rank, boasted that he was Caesar and would keep faith.[66] Moreover, in the nation *fides* was the quality most important in Rome's dealings with foreign powers. As it was part of *virtus* in the individual to observe the obligations of *fides* by aiding his clients and political associates, so it was part of *virtus* in the nation as a whole to deal justly with its allies, to observe *fides* and justice towards them.[67] In the passage of time, as Rome's power grew, her allies first in Italy and then overseas, although nominally her equals, came to be treated as her clients who owed unquestioning obedience to their patron, until to entrust themselves to the *fides* of Rome came to mean unconditional surrender.[68]

The Roman aristocrat was expected to show courage and wisdom, the two qualities most important for a general and a magistrate. In this context wisdom did not denote a rarified philosophic detachment or an intellectual enquiry into first causes and the nature of things. It meant practical political judgement, which was of little use unless expressed in words at meetings of the Roman People and of the Senate in such a way as to influence the course of events. It was only thus, by originating and instigating public policy, by being an *auctor publici consilii*, that the Roman politician could attain the highest form of prestige, *auctoritas*.[69] Consequently L. Caecilius Metellus aimed not merely at possessing the highest wisdom but also at being the best orator. Cicero was later, not wholly disingenuously, to rank distinction in oratory with nobility of birth and military service as one of the three claims to the consulship. As in all aspects of the aristocratic ideal, there is a dualism. The service of the state went hand in hand with self-interest. An excellent orator used his gift to further the interests of the Republic and to advance his own cause among his fellow nobles by gaining clients and by defending his political allies and attacking his enemies by skilful advocacy in the law-courts. But mere technical expertise was not enough. As Plautus put it, 'men of action are of much more use to the people than men who are eloquent and clever. *Virtus* easily finds its own fluent eloquence. A citizen who is eloquent without *virtus* I consider as like a hired mourner who praises others but cannot truthfully praise herself.'[70] Oratory, like all other attributes and possessions, was praiseworthy only so far as it was founded on and sprang from *virtus*, the service of the state and the observation of the moral code. In a word, the orator must be *bonus*, in all its senses.[71]

The interdependence of the doing of great deeds and the observance of a proper standard of conduct comes out clearly in the use of the plural form, *virtutes*. *Virtutes* are 'things well done', *bene facta*. This basic notion was extended in two ways by stressing either the participle or the adverb. Thus *virtutes* are, on the one hand, great deeds, on the other, a right standard of conduct. Plautus, for instance, makes slave say to slave 'heavens, you couldn't praise as I could your *virtutes*, your evil deeds at home and abroad'.[72] This is comic language and Plautus mocks an aristocratic formula—*domi duellique bene facta*. Elsewhere he used *virtutes* to denote great deeds of valour: 'Mars wouldn't dare to speak or to compare his *virtutes* with yours', and a high standard of conduct as when in the *Miles Gloriosus* the old man Periplectomenus is interrupted in a lengthy description of the amatory pursuits of his youth by the aside 'O charming semi-ancient, if you possessed the *virtutes* which you relate.'[73] What is in question here is not the achievement of mighty deeds of love nor virtues in the abstract ethical sense, but a proper standard of conduct and practice, a code of manners and etiquette: 'I never seduced another man's whore at a party'—gentlemanly conduct indeed!

Thus the ideal of the Roman aristocracy in its earliest expression known to us. It consisted in the gaining of pre-eminent *gloria* by the winning of public office and the participation in public life and by using these methods to achieve great deeds in the service of the state. It concerned not only the individual noble but the whole family, not only its living members but the dead ancestors and the unborn posterity. It imposed a proper standard of conduct. In its strict application it was a concept at once extrovert and exclusive: extrovert in its insistence on action, on deeds; exclusive in its concern for the family and in that the service of the state alone was considered a fit field for the exercise of a noble's talents. Outside the service of the Republic there existed no public office and, therefore, strictly speaking, no *gloria*, no *nobilitas*, no *auctoritas*, no *virtus*. The origins of this ideal may lie far back in the past history of the Republic from which no contemporary record survives. But Plautus' exuberant use of the complex of ideas surrounding the concept of *virtus* for both direct and extended reference and for oblique allusion, both for topical comment and comic effect, may reflect a condition and a time when the political vocabulary of the Roman aristocracy was being more closely defined.[74] His constant employment of these terms may indicate an intellectual climate in which such ideas were frequently in men's minds and on men's lips. The latter part of Plautus' career saw the bitter internal struggles of the Roman nobility which followed the Hannibalic war and which culminated in the attacks on the Cornelii Scipiones and the exile of Scipio Africanus. These struggles called into question many of the fundamental attitudes of the aristocracy and probably imposed a closer definition of the terminology. This terminology, it will have been seen, was built up by giving special meanings and emphases to words and concepts taken from the common stock. Inevitably the particular and the general, the special and the ordinary could not be kept distinct. By the time of Terence and of Lucilius the special aristocratic definitions had become conventional, had passed back into common speech.[75]

The ideal of the Roman oligarchy not only became accepted as the ideal of Rome herself but exercised a decisive influence on the development of an important section of the Latin language and of the thought of the Romans.

Constantly this complex of ideas has been described as peculiarly Roman. How far was it influenced by Greek thought and philosophy? In a sense, the question and its answer do not matter. Whatever its origin and subsequent development, the *virtus* complex was regarded by the Romans themselves as embodying the specially Roman ideal. But since direct Greek influence has been detected, since it has been held that in the latter half of the second century BC traditionally Roman ideals were redefined on the basis of Greek Stoicism, we may conclude with a glance at an interesting psychological manifestation, the proper history of which has yet to be written, namely, the curiously ambivalent attitude of the Romans to things Greek.[76]

Although Rome had been in direct or indirect contact with Greece almost since the foundation of the city, although by the end of the third century BC Plautus could present Latin adaptations of Greek plays and Q. Fabius Pictor write a history of Rome in Greek, it was not until the first half of the second century that the two civilizations met face to face. The influx into Rome during this period of Asiatic luxury and Greek manners on a scale far greater than anything that had gone before provoked, according to our tradition, a double reaction. On the one hand, the youth of the city, particularly the young men of aristocratic family, eagerly embraced the innovations and tended to abandon the traditional Roman morality for display and vice, to reject the laws and the magistrates for philosophical speculation. On the other hand, the main body of senators, with Cato and Scipio Aemilianus especially prominent in our tradition, strove to maintain the *mos maiorum* by accepting those imports which could be made to conform to it and rejecting those which did not. Cato will concern us in another context in the next chapter, but it is worthwhile here to examine Scipio's attitude in some detail, since he, if anyone, at this time might be claimed as a liberal. By birth and adoption he was placed in the very centre of the Roman oligarchy; from his early years he was exposed to Greek influence.[77]

Of Scipio's speeches only some score of fragments remain. Of them the earliest which are of significance date from the censorship which, amid the pressures of military difficulties in Spain and of a crisis in recruiting at home, he conducted with unusual severity in 142 BC. When his colleague tried to moderate his severity, Scipio attacked him publicly and savagely. Whether he had a colleague or not, he said, he would conduct everything in accordance with the majesty of the Republic.[78] He seems at once to have made his attitude clear in a speech exhorting the Roman People to observe the *mos maiorum*.[79] In this speech he listed examples of previous censorial severity and referred with approval to the censorship of Cato. The body of the speech was an attack on the many ways in which ancestral standards were being flouted. This was a theme to which Scipio returned again and again in his later speeches. He castigated the vice and prodigality of P. Sulpicius Gallus and Ti. Claudius Asellus, the avarice of L. Aurelius Cotta, the degeneracy of the noble youth in general who practised pursuits 'which our ancestors decided were to be considered shameful for free men'.[80] In this speech and in that against Gallus it was precisely the corrupting influence of Greek morals and customs that Scipio attacked. He hammered his point home by the abusive use of Greek words.[81] In other words, Scipio reacted in no way differently from the rest of the moralizing tradition. That he may have been pursuing his own political interests in these speeches is largely irrelevant: it is his choice of stick to beat his enemies that is significant.

As for Scipio's career before he became an established politician, we have already mentioned the famous story of how he sought the help and advice of Polybius on how to become worthy of the great traditions of his family and to meet the demands of the code of his class.[82] Polybius, we are told, promised Scipio every assistance towards enabling him to speak and act in a way worthy of his ancestors. Consequently Scipio directed himself to obtaining a reputation for wise moderation and in doing so set himself against the vice and Greek laxity which then flourished among the noble youth. Next he studied to excel his contemporaries in liberality and honesty about money. Finally he gained a reputation for courage by hunting both in Macedonia, whither he had been taken by his father, L. Aemilius Paullus, and where he won a certain reputation in battle, and at Rome. At Rome, in contrast to his contemporaries who busied themselves with trials and *salutationes*, the formal receptions at which members of the nobility received their clients and associates, Scipio by his dash and bravery was always doing something glorious and worthy of remark. Thus he won a finer reputation than the rest.

If this story tells us anything about Scipio, it is his acceptance of the demands of the aristocratic tradition. The complaints against him were based on his divergence from the duties it imposed and his subsequent actions were devoted to making himself worthy of it. Scipio agreed with his contemporaries about the end to be reached. He differed from them only in the way in which he was to reach this end. They reached it by the traditional path of speaking in the law-courts. He, because of personal aversion, substituted a method of training and winning public notice of his own. The essential difference between Scipio and his contemporaries lay in the field in which he achieved the great deeds on which *gloria* rested. Polybius tells us as much: 'So in a little while he outran his contemporaries to a greater extent than is recorded of any other Roman, although he followed a different path to glory from all the others in accordance with Roman tradition and custom.' Even such minor nonconformity would have been denied to a man who lacked Scipio's birth and position. There is no suggestion that even Scipio, once he had attained a pre-eminent position among his contemporaries, would not have followed the normal career of public office. As it turned out, however, when, after military service in Spain and Africa from 151 to 148 BC, he returned to Rome to stand for the aedileship, he was by popular demand exempted from the laws, elected consul and assigned the province of Africa without lot. He then proceeded to the destruction of Carthage. There is no evidence that he undertook the task unwillingly or that he shared the fears of his kinsman Scipio Nasica. Later, in Spain, he likewise showed himself the faithful servant of the Senate. That Scipio was a reluctant conqueror, opposed to Rome's imperialistic expansion, is a romantic fiction. His contemporaries knew otherwise: at his funeral it was said 'it was inevitable that empire should exist where he was'.[83] Nor was his obedience to Roman tradition tempered by un-Roman humanity. His father, L. Aemilius Paullus, both in Macedonia and Epirus faithfully observed the interests of Rome and committed in consequence many acts of great cruelty. Scipio followed his father's example at Carthage and at Numantia. At the triumphal games after the destruction of Carthage he had deserters thrown to the beasts.

Scipio was interested and trained in Greek studies, yet in his public life he based his actions on Roman tradition. As a young man he accommodated himself to this tradition; as a civil magistrate he attempted to recall the People to the *mos maiorum*; as a military commander he obeyed the traditional authority of the Senate; as a private person he delighted in philosophical discussion with Polybius, Panaetius and the other members of his circle of friends. Even Cicero, who looked back to the age of Scipio as a golden age and made it the setting of a number of philosophical and rhetorical dialogues, observed the dichotomy between Roman tradition and the doctrines of Greek philosophy. Both he considered valuable and praiseworthy, but if a choice had to be made he was quite clear that the life of a statesman in the ancestral tradition was far preferable, although the man in whom both were present was worthy of the highest honour and respect. Scipio, Laelius, Philus and Cato too were statesmen and politicians according to the *mos maiorum*. They were also all interested in Greek culture. The two acted together to produce an exceptional nobility of character, but the practice of politics and statecraft was not affected by the theories of philosophy.[84] In discussion on political philosophy and the theory of the state Scipio, according to Cicero, maintained 'that by far the best condition of organized society is that which our ancestors have handed down to us'. Scipio was no different in this respect from Cato who for Cicero and others was the very epitome of ancient Roman *virtus*. The tradition in Cicero and Plutarch that Cato learnt Greek only in his old age is both inherently improbable and contradicted by Plutarch himself when he said that he thought Cato's writings showed Greek influence (which is confirmed by the extant fragments of Cato's writings and speeches) and that in 190 BC Cato could have addressed the Athenians in Greek but preferred Latin. Cicero classes him with Scipio and his friends as a man both possessed of outstanding natural talents and influenced by the tenets of Greek philosophy. The career and attitudes of the young Scipio and old Cato touched at many points. Both strove to preserve the *mos maiorum*. As censor Scipio identified himself with the severity that Cato had shown in the same office. The two men co-operated to secure the return of the Achaean exiles. Cato was the foremost advocate, Scipio the agent of the destruction of Carthage. Both were interested in and conscious of the benefits of Greek culture, but in public life both rested their actions and speeches firmly on the sure ground of the Roman tradition. In all this Cato and Scipio were no different from most educated senators in second-century Rome.[85]

Further, when Roman tradition and Greek philosophy met, it was the latter that made concessions. In 154 BC Cato agitated for the dismissal from Rome of the Athenian envoys, Diogenes, Critolaus and Carneades, so that the youth of the city, infected with a passion for philosophizing, should once more obey the laws and the magistrates.[86] Cato was not alone in his uneasiness: the Senate ejected the ambassadors. Yet at the same time, a time moreover of considerable unrest at Rome, Polybius enjoyed the close friendship of Scipio and ten years later Panaetius, like Polybius, a Greek and a philosopher as well, spent two years with Scipio unmolested by anyone. Panaetius, it is true, seems to have moved only in aristocratic circles and not to have held public lectures on his ideas. But there was another factor in his immunity. Panaetius and, later, Poseidonius succeeded at Rome only because they adapted their philosophy to the demands of the Roman tradition, rejecting whatever ran counter to it, as, for instance, the doctrines of the inherent superiority of monarchy and of the brotherhood of man. A particularly clear example is that most dangerous of all subjects for a Greek philosopher at Rome, Roman imperialism. Carneades, one of those expelled in 154, denied the existence of natural justice as a basis of law and thus held that Roman imperialism could not philosophically be justified. It was, he argued, unjust, based merely on expediency and the power of the stronger. On the other hand, Panaetius, a Stoic and therefore committed to belief in an absolute fundamental justice, could handle the question without offence to Roman susceptibilities. Domination being the right of the better not the stronger, Roman imperialism was justified by its benefits to the conquered. Panaetius, Polybius and Poseidonius were convinced that Rome was called for world domination and, therefore, had moral obligations to her subjects. Imperialism had its duties and these extended not merely to material welfare but to intellectual and moral good. But in order to reach this conclusion, Panaetius had to modify Stoicism in at least one important particular. The old Stoics were concerned with the individual, not the state. Panaetius placed the individual in the framework of the state: no ideal state either, but the actual Roman Republic which was justified by being based on the universal law of human society. Though this evolution in Stoicism may have been helped by other factors such as the teaching of the utilitarian and positivistic Carneades, we may see here the influence of the unmoving weight of the Roman tradition. From Polybius and Panaetius the moral justification of imperialism passed to Poseidonius and Cicero. But although this Stoic idea, redefined to fit the Roman situation, passed into the intellectual *koine* at Rome, there is no evidence that it had any influence whatever on Republican political practice.[87]

The typical attitude of the Roman nobility in the second century BC was to combine interest in Greek culture with strict adherence to traditional aims and standards. Foreign influences and importations were admissible only if they remained matters of private interest and did not violate tradition or endanger the state. In religion the state was directly involved since the state religion was conceived only as one aspect of the government of the Republic. In 205 BC Rome was seized by a religious panic to allay which the *Mater Idaea* was brought from Pessinus to Rome. The importation of the goddess was an act of public policy, deliberated on and carried out by the Senate. It soon became evident that the worship of the Great Mother involved orgiastic practices. The new cult was found to conflict with *mos maiorum* and the Senate promptly decreed that no Roman citizen should take part in the rites.[88] Similarly the Bacchic cult was considered a conspiracy against the safety of the state. It was held to endanger the traditional moral code, traditional civil authority, traditional religion.[89] More drastic action was considered necessary than against the cult of the Great Mother, but the Bacchic worship was not totally suppressed. Continuance of the cult was allowed though under such strict supervision and regulation that celebration of its rites was made as difficult as possible. But the important point is that once the Bacchic cult had been made to conform with *mos maiorum*, the Senate was prepared to allow the worship to continue. As in religion so in culture, as witness, on the one hand, the expulsion of Diogenes, Critolaus and Carneades and, on the other, the acceptance of Panaetius and Polybius. Philosophy was all very well for Greek boys; Roman youths should listen to the laws and the magistrates. Again, in 154 BC Scipio Nasica prevented the building of a permanent theatre at Rome, although the contracts had already been placed, on the grounds that such a thing was useless and harmful to public morals.[90]

The foreign importations of the second century BC produced a consistent reaction at Rome: a desire to preserve the traditional Roman respect for authority, the established state religion and the public morality. As with all innovations the test was the *mos maiorum*. Those importations which could be made to conform with it were accepted; those which would not or could not make the necessary adjustment were suppressed or expelled. Greek culture became part of the educational equipment of the upper class, but for the public at large Greek ideas were considered dangerous. Subversive notions were not to be spread abroad and even among the nobility, where they could be admitted, a firm distinction was to be observed between private cultural interests and public political action. This ambivalent attitude of Rome to

Greece became fixed and persistent. On the one hand, the whole Greek apparatus of cultured and civilized life in art and literature, in thought and ideas, even in manners and dress was eagerly sought and eagerly accepted. On the other, to condemn an object, an idea, a custom as Greek was for long the last resource of Roman contempt.

CHAPTER II

THE NEW MEN

'*Since* nobilitas *is nothing other than* virtus *given recognition, who looks for antiquity of lineage in a man whom you see growing old in glory?*'[1]

MORE THAN ANY other single individual, M. Porcius Cato may be held responsible for the tradition of the second century as it has come down to us.[2] Born at Tusculum about 234 BC, brought up on a farm in the Sabine country, introduced into public life at Rome by the patrician L. Valerius Flaccus, Cato achieved the consulship of 195 BC and the censorship of 184. Throughout his long life (he died in 149) he was the self-appointed guardian of the aristocratic conscience. In his historical work, the *Origines*, published in its final form in his old age, he glorified the great deeds of the *respublica* by omitting the names of the individual noble commanders.[3] Nevertheless, he held up for admiration men like the obscure tribune of the soldiers, Q. Caedicius, who acted in a way worthy of the aristocratic ideal.[4] Caedicius, by his courage and devotion to the *respublica* saved the Roman army and received from the gods a reward commensurate with his *virtus*. He alone of his band of five hundred survived to serve the Republic afterwards bravely and actively.[5] Cato took the opportunity of redressing previous neglect and of giving the man at last his due measure of praise. But as Cato put the exploits of individuals into the context of the *respublica*, so he put Rome into the context of Italy. Two of the seven books of his work were devoted to the *populi et boni et strenui* of Italy.[6] He praised their discipline and way of life and, more than this, he held that the Romans had derived their character from the harsh discipline and *mores* of the Sabines.[7] His attack on the Roman aristocracy did not come obliquely merely by the exaltation of the *respublica* and the insistence on the contribution of Italy. He inserted some of his own speeches accusing the nobility of cupidity and oppression, as when he argued for leniency for the Rhodians or attacked Ser. Sulpicius Galba.[8] Feminine luxury also came to his stern notice and the decay of ancestral custom and religious observance.[9] Similarly throughout his career in many public speeches he attacked the prevailing low standards of public and private morality, the abandonment by the nobility of its own high ideal. Cruelty and oppression, vice and, above all, breaches of the cardinal virtue of *fides* met bitter condemnation.[10] So too did men who falsely claimed *gloria* which they had not won, who invented battles or exaggerated victories, who even decorated the walls of their houses with spoils not captured from the enemy, but bought.[11] The abuse of wealth was a constant preoccupation to Cato, whether it manifested itself in avarice or venality or luxury. 'Thieves who steal private possessions', he said, 'spend their lives in chains and fetters; those who plunder the public treasury live amid gold and purple.'[12] Of an objectionable tribune he remarked that he could be bought for a crust of bread to speak or keep silent.[13] He inveighed against those who 'purchased honour but did not redeem their evil deeds by good'.[14] True honour and glory sprang from good deeds and from *virtus*: they were not to be won by conspicuous expenditure of money.[15] Legislation to reduce conspicuous expenditure or conspicuous consumption, feminine arrogance or feminine self-indulgence always found Cato an advocate ready with a loud voice and powerful lungs.[16] Luxury and ostentation in building and furniture excited Cato's contempt; so did undue attention to cuisine.[17] 'There exists', he asserted, 'a great interest in food, a great indifference to *virtus*' and he held that it was difficult for a city to be safe in which a fish cost more than an ox.

In all his attacks Cato asserted the aristocratic ideal of *virtus* and *gloria*, *bene facta* and the service of the state.[18] Ancestral standards were appealed to and the obligations of *fides* laid down.[19] Thus far there is little difference between Cato's attitude and that of Scipio Aemilianus. They agreed that the decay of ancient standards whether in the government of the provinces abroad or in private life at home was a danger to the state and must be stopped. But between the two men an important difference existed. When Scipio recalled the Roman People to the ancestral ways, he spoke of a tradition which was to him, an Aemilius by birth and a Cornelius Scipio by adoption, immediate and personal. The line of his own ancestors stretched far back into Roman history. Cato, however, was a new man and a new man, precisely, lacked ancestors in the special sense of the Roman political tradition. Consequently although we find him appealing to the *mos maiorum* and even praising his own father, it was on his own achievements and his own standards that he took his stand.[20] He recorded at length on diverse occasions his devotion to the interests of the state: he had never distributed either his own money or that of his friends from a desire for power and office; he had never imposed Roman governors on allied towns to plunder their goods and their children; he had never confined distribution of booty taken from the enemy to his own immediate friends so as to defraud the soldiers who had captured it; he had never made friends with the rich by robbing the state; on the contrary, he used his own money to serve the Republic and his efforts to save the city.[21] To his consulship in Spain, he put on record, he took but few servants; on the journey thither he drank the same wine as the slaves who rowed the ship; rather than cause the state unnecessary expense he abandoned his war-horse when he left the country.[22] His training of his armies and his discipline were stern and exemplary.[23] Similarly in his private life he boasted that he possessed no costly building, vase or piece of clothing, no valuable male or female slave. If he had something to use, he used it; if he had not, he did without.[24] Plutarch records his saying: 'I prefer to compete with the best about *virtus*, not with the rich about riches or with the avaricious about avarice.'[25] The *virtus* he preferred to struggle over was something personal and individual. Office was won by an individual's *mores*: glory and honour too were personal, based on an individual's achievements.[26] The play made by the nobility with the glory of their ancestors was irrelevant. What mattered in the final assessment were the actions and standards of the individual. The long line of ancestors boasted by a corrupt noble was of no account beside Cato's own youth spent in learning the harsh lessons of abstinence, thrift and hard work in the Sabine country.[27]

A new man attacking the established aristocracy from the position of his own achievements, his own standards, his own *virtus*: the figure is most familiar to us from the writers of the first century BC, especially from Cicero and Sallust, both of whom came from backgrounds similar to Cato's to Rome, the one to the consulate, a position in the state and glory in literature, the other to the frustration of ambition and the writing of history.

It is in Cicero that we first meet clearly and unequivocally stated the proposition that *virtus* was the quality peculiar to the *novus homo* in the same way that *nobilitas* was peculiar to the noble. Thus in the peroration to the speech *Pro Sestio* we read 'and as for you young men, those of you who are noble I would stir up to imitate your ancestors, those of you who can obtain nobility by *virtus* and innate ability I would exhort to that way of life in which many new men have flourished in honour and glory'.[28] The contrast that Cicero made was essentially between two different concepts of nobility, one deriving from all the apparatus of hereditary aristocracy, the other from the personal achievements and standards of the individual. Theoretically and legally, all Roman citizens of appropriate age, character and past office were eligible for the consulship. Theoretically, too, the new man who attained the consulship ennobled both himself and his family forever, like Cato who, according to Cicero, 'considered that his *virtus*, not his lineage, commended him to the Roman People and wished the beginning of his lineage and name to spring and derive from himself'.[29] In fact, the new men of the first century maintained or are represented as having maintained, that the *nobiles* had become an exclusive clique, that the descendants of consulars alone, or at least the sons of senators, were considered fit for the consulship, that all others were disqualified by reason of their birth.[30] *Nobilitas*, it was said, rested, according to the nobles themselves, on birth and family, not on individual worth and achievement, on *genus*, not on *virtus*. Cicero, claiming to speak for the new men generally, protested against this view.[31] *Virtus*, not ancestry, was the proper criterion of a man's worthiness for all office, including the consulship. A man was worthy of *nobilitas* because of character not his caste, *moribus non maioribus*.[32] Moreover, Cicero insisted, this was the ancient and original concept of nobility: the contemporary insistence on ancestors and family was a perversion of the old ideal.[33] The new men claimed to be following the same path to nobility as the great *nobiles* of the past and thus to have an affinity with them equal to that of their descendants by blood and family, to be, that is, the true successors to the old aristocracy.[34]

The issue was put unmistakably by Sallust in the speech which, in his monograph on the Jugurthine war, he attributed to Marius. The theme of the speech is, precisely, the contrast between Marius himself, the new man, and the hereditary nobility. On the one side were ancient nobility, the brave deeds of their ancestors, the resources of their relatives and connections, extensive *clientelae*, all the advantages of wealth, a famous pedigree and the offices of state which the *nobiles* sought as though they were theirs by right.[35] On the other stood Marius alone, relying on his own toils and dangers, his own military exploits and the scars he bore on the front of his body, on those things most beneficial to the state which he had learnt by personal and bitter experience, not from reading the history of his ancestors and Greek textbooks. In short, Marius took his stand upon his own *bene facta rei publicae*, his own standards, his own *virtus*.[36] These formed Marius' lineage, these formed his nobility, not left by inheritance, like the advantages of the nobility, but won by his own personal toils and dangers.[37] *Nobilitas*, Sallust made Marius assert, sprang from *virtus*. But *virtus*, as he meant it, was personal and individual. It alone could be neither given nor received as a gift.[38] It had nothing to do with ancestors and family position. Therefore, *nobilitas* was personal and individual also. Ancestors and family position might inspire a man, but they had nothing to do with *virtus* and, consequently, nothing to do with *nobilitas* either, for *nobilitas* arose not from birth or wealth but from individual worth. As Marius put it: 'Although I regard all men's natures as equal and alike, nevertheless I regard the bravest as the best born'.[39] Since all men shared the same nature, it was the use that each made of his natural gifts that determined his *virtus* and thus his claim to *nobilitas*. Like Cicero, Sallust made Marius claim that this was the concept of nobility held by the old aristocracy.[40] The *nobiles* of his own day were mistaken in their reliance on *vetus nobilitas*. Their ancestors had bequeathed them what they could: riches, their images, their glorious memory. *Virtus* they could not possibly bequeath.[41] The true successors to the old nobles were not their blood descendants, but men like Marius, for, since *virtus* was not inheritable, neither was true *nobilitas*.[42]

The views that Sallust here attributed to Marius have obvious relation to the thought of the *novi homines* of the last years of the Republic as presented by Cicero. How far they represent the thoughts of the historical Marius is difficult to determine. Sallust's own narrative makes it clear that up to his legateship in Numidia Marius had taken no part in the activities of the group of politicians, represented in our tradition by Memmius and Mamilius, which had begun to agitate against the nobility.[43] On the contrary, there is reason to believe that up to that time Marius had been a comparatively undistinguished hanger-on of the Caecilii Metelli and broke with them only when his ambition was opposed. In making this break Marius, as depicted by Sallust, was motivated not by any concern for the rights and claims of new men, but solely by his own monstrous desire for the consulship. His subsequent seditious intrigues against his commander arose from this desire and they were successful not so much from any merit in Marius as from his putting himself forward at a time when the common people was excited by Mamilius' agitation and the business men were dissatisfied with the conduct of the war. Sallust's whole tendency is to show Marius as concerned only with his own personal advantage and as exploiting the dissatisfactions at Rome to serve it. Even Marius' innovation in the recruitment of the army Sallust interpreted in a pejorative sense. Marius appealed for honour and position to the lowest classes. For a man in search of power the poorest were the most useful since they had no respect for property and regarded as honourable anything for which they were paid.[44] It must indeed be remarked that in the nine years of Marius' predominance only one other new man, Flavius Fimbria, reached the consulship. According to Cicero, Marius' position actually prevented another *novus*, C. Billienus, from attaining this office.[45] It is not easy to believe that Marius stood for the principle of a career open to personal talent.

Sallust, however, was not much concerned with the career of the historical Marius.[46] His business was with an abstraction, a type: the *novus homo* of unspoilt character and brilliant attainments opposed and corrupted by the exclusive arrogance of the nobility. This formed the particular example of his general statement about the attitude of the nobility to the consulship and their considering it polluted if held by a new man.[47] The historian was repeating a propaganda tag, not presenting historical analysis. The whole episode of Metellus and Marius, in fact, is a propaganda cliché. The remark about the nobility's hold on the consulship and its pollution if held by a *novus* is as accurate an item of historical analysis as the parallel statement that the *plebs* had an equal hold on the other magistracies, as serious a piece of constitutional comment as Catiline's description of Cicero as a foreign citizen of Rome or the jibe of L. Manlius Torquatus that Cicero was the third foreign king of Rome after Tarquinius and Numa.[48]

Nevertheless, although the exact formulation of the speech was doubtless Sallust's own and drew on the polemic of the end of the Republic, Marius' claim that the nobles were degenerate and no longer fit to rule may represent his general line of propaganda. Cicero records that Marius attacked birth and privilege and defied the *dignitas* of the nobility.[49] But Cicero in his formulation of the propaganda of the new men reveals a significant fact about them. By his time the original concept of *virtus* had become debased by continuous and indiscriminate use.[50] In redefining it, Cicero, like Cato a century earlier, was concerned not with the destruction of the old, but with purging and strengthening it. He was prepared to admit nobility of birth as one of the claims to the consulship beside those of the new men based on a personal *virtus*. He wished not so much to replace the old idea of *nobilitas* as to widen it to include both the noble with his inherited position and the new man with his individual merit. He and the other new men desired parity with and recognition by the nobility, not to supersede them. In this Cicero seems to have represented the aspirations of the new men with some accuracy. Although they attacked the nobility for its improper acquisition and improper use of political power, for its perversion of *clientelae* and marriage alliances, for its arrogance and *nobilitas*, although in contrast they extolled and praised their own achievements, their own harsh and rustic upbringing, their own uprightness and virtue, their aim was not to destroy or supplant the nobility. This is clear of Marius no less than of Cato the censor. A client of the Caecilii Metelli, Marius broke with them when his ambition was thwarted and won the consulship by a combination of seditious intrigue, blatant demagogy and luck. To meet the menace of the elusive and uncertain Cimbri and Teutones he was given, with the approval of the Senate, a whole series of consulships. Neither a democrat nor a revolutionary, his aim was to build up a personal following to balance the inherited *clientelae* of the nobles, to be recognized and accepted by the nobles as their equal, to become, as an ex-consul and ex-censor, a senior statesman and a director of senatorial policy.[51] In the end he was to take a terrible vengeance in proscription and massacre on the *nobiles* who had supported, used and then discarded him.[52] In the Ciceronian age the pressure of the new men was more insistent. The effects of the enfranchisement of Italy began to make themselves felt and the emerging monarchic faction leaders, first Sulla and then Pompey and Caesar, offered wider opportunities for self-advancement.[53] But the real revolutionaries of the age were not the new men, not even merely noble: they tended to come from the most ancient and reverend section of the Roman aristocracy. Ap. Claudius Pulcher, the leader of the faction of Ti. Gracchus, L. Cornelius Sulla and M. Aemilius Lepidus, L. Sergius Catilina and C. Iulius Caesar—all were Patricians. In strong contrast stands Pompey, whose family, although noble for three generations, was despised and hated by the good men of the governing oligarchy.[54] His youth was spent in prosecuting through illegality and fraud, treachery and bloodshed the interests of Sulla and his own advancement. His maturity was consumed by a struggle to win recognition of his pre-eminence and acceptance by Sulla's oligarchy and its successors. Returning from the East he ostentatiously refused to imitate Sulla and sought accommodation and connection with the younger Cato. Cato's rebuff drove him into alliance with Caesar, from which he almost immediately tried to extricate himself and with which he was never easy. In the end it was the threat of Caesar in Gaul and the imminence of civil war which drove Cato and his faction, whose pretensions Pompey had overshadowed, whose relatives he had murdered and whose alliance he had desired, to accept and use him. It was their fault the accommodation was so late in coming. Ambitious and bloodthirsty, untrustworthy and devious, Pompey was yet no revolutionary.[55]

The new men of the end of the Roman Republic summed up their position in a reinterpretation of the old aristocratic concept of *virtus*. It is Sallust who discloses most clearly how this redefinition was made. The aristocratic ideal, as we have seen, consisted in the winning of *gloria* by the commission of examplary deeds according to a proper standard of conduct in the service of the state. It was extrovert in that it emphasized action and conduct, exclusive in that it was restricted to one class engaged in one activity. In his historical works Sallust's attitude centred on a concept of *virtus* as the functioning of *ingenium*, a man's innate talent, to achieve exemplary deeds and thus win *gloria* through a proper standard of behaviour. This concept, clearly, is a direct development from the aristocratic ideal.[56] But there is one vital difference: the place assigned to *ingenium*. It is obvious that an aristocrat would be expected to employ his inborn talent, his nature, his *ingenium*, to its fullest extent in his service of the state. But although in a few passages the term does occur in company with peculiarly aristocratic concepts and formulations, it did not acquire a quasi-technical sense nor had it a precise place in the aristocratic ideal.[57] For Sallust, on the other hand, *ingenium* was vital for two reasons. Firstly, it was the state of *ingenium* which determined the moral content of *virtus*. True *virtus* not only lay in the achievement of great and glorious deeds: it demanded also a good *ingenium* expressed in moral actions. Secondly, a concept of *virtus* based ultimately on the nature of each individual necessarily lacked the exclusiveness characteristic of the aristocratic ideal, which, almost by definition, was restricted to the *respublica* and the *nobiles*. Consequently Sallust's concept of *virtus* applied to every field of activity and to every class of people. Any man engaged on any activity could claim *virtus* if he exerted his talents to the full, performed gloriously and observed the rules of morality. Sallust, however, accepted that of all the works that *ingenium* could achieve the highest was the service of the state, with the writing of history a poor second.[58] If the service of the state was the highest field for the exercise of talent, it followed that the highest glory and the truest *virtus* were those which arose from this activity. It is at this point that the political significance of Sallust's inclusive concept becomes apparent. Although he agreed with the aristocratic tradition that for practical purposes *virtus* was the prerogative of men engaged in public life, he did not follow this tradition in restricting it to any one class or group. The exercise of *ingenium* in the service of the *respublica* was open to all: *virtus* admitted *nobiles* and *novi homines* alike. But, since *virtus* was personal, the nobility to which it gave rise was also personal, not inheritable.

Towards the end of the second century BC contemporaries had alleged that the nobility had declined from its earlier high standards of conduct, to which both Scipio Aemilianus and Cato the Censor strove to recall it. In the much more radically changed circumstances of the last years of the Republic reassertion, it was held, was not enough: the old tradition had to be reinterpreted and redefined to suit the needs of different times and different men. The nobility was represented as having lost all ability or right to govern. Therefore a new concept of *nobilitas* was required in which the criterion was not birth and ancestry but individual worth and achievement. Sallust's handling of the concept of *virtus* shows most clearly how this was accomplished and it takes its place beside Cicero's redefinitions of other traditional concepts such as *mos maiorum*.[59]

We are here, once again, moving in the sphere not of objective constitutional analysis but of political polemic. The Romans themselves held that the tribunate of Ti. Gracchus began the revolution by splitting the state into two parties, later termed Optimates and Populares.[60] The notion must be handled with caution. It is necessary first to think away any idea of political parties on the modern model, Conservative and Labour, Democrat and Republican. We are used to the two-party system, but it has no place in Roman politics in any age. Nor have the terms Optimates and Populares very much to do with differences of political principle. Both were concerned only to win political power. The Optimates are in some ways the more easily approachable. They at least have shape and form. In the main they were Sulla's oligarchy and its descendants, centring on the family of the Caecilii Metelli, and led in the last age of the Republic by a man who never became consul, the younger M. Porcius Cato. The word Populares, on the other hand, if it does not denote a party, does not even identify a specific group of men. The term is applied to individuals, to measures, to policies, not to a fixed group. Essentially it describes a particular method of propaganda and political working. The Populares looked back to the Gracchi and based their power on the power of the Roman People. There were in the Roman state, in theory at least, two principles of authority: the *libertas* of a supposedly sovereign People and the *auctoritas* of the Senate. The Populares used and appealed to the former, the Optimates to the latter. The *auctoritas* of the Senate was naturally managed in the interests of the group in possession. *Libertas*, likewise, was a political catchword, invoked to excuse the search for power and domination.[61] It was on this plea that the young Pompey raised a private army and rescued Rome and Italy from the domination of the Marian faction. Caesar the proconsul, outmanœuvred and trapped by Pompey and the faction of Cato, turned his army against the government 'in order to liberate himself and the Roman People from the domination of a faction'.[62] The defenders of the liberty of the People were traditionally the tribunes of the plebs. Therefore we find the Populares working through the assemblies of the Roman People, using tribunes and invoking in their propaganda all the ideas associated with the liberty of the People and tribunician rights. In assailing their opponents they claimed to champion the demands of new men against the arrogant exclusiveness of the faction of the oligarchy. But the Populares were anything but democrats. Indeed, a man might be a Popularis, that is, employ a certain political method and style, at one point only in his career or on one issue only. Very few Roman politicians were consistent Populares. In opposition, the Optimates appealed to the authority, prestige and prerogatives of the Senate. But, again, there was no division into nobles and people, senatorials and democrats. Optimates and Populares were alike members of the Senate, alike members of the nobility. The political struggles after Sulla, like those before, concerned the ruling aristocracy. The only difference was that they went different ways to work. As Sallust, writing of the upheavals of the last age of the Republic, put it: 'All those who convulsed the state alleged the public good under fair names, some that they were defending the rights of the People, others that the authority of the Senate should predominate. In fact each was striving for his own power. Neither showed restraint or moderation in the struggle. Both used their victories for oppression.'[63]

Sallust, writing in the Triumviral period, went further than Cicero. He applied his concept of *virtus* both to the broad sweep of Roman history from its beginnings to his own times and to the particular facts of the Jugurthine war and the conspiracy of Catiline.[64] From this application he was concerned to demonstrate that both the oligarchs and their enemies who attacked their pretensions and aspired to their position had betrayed the ideals they professed. As a political thinker Sallust was incompetent, as an historian variously delinquent.[65] Yet his basic notion, that the failure of the Roman Republic was connected with a failure in the ideal of *virtus*, was not without merit. Although the way Sallust applied this basic idea leaves much to be desired and although, like most other Roman historians, he was obsessed with morality, the apparent moral platitudes mask a political reality. It is valid to analyse the breakdown of the Republic in terms of the perversion of the ideal of *virtus*, whereby personal power and position were sought at the expense and, ultimately, to the destruction of the Commonwealth. Every generation of the Republic could show examples of oppression abroad and arrogance at home, of neglect of duty and of self-regarding ambition. The historians and moralists loved to depict, although they could not agree on the date, an age of perfect harmony, total virtue and complete devotion to the state. It had, of course, never existed. Yet it is true that for long years the defects of individuals were contained by the strength of the tradition. As late as the early decades of the second century BC the demands of the aristocratic tradition could be felt as imperative. Scipio Africanus, assailed by his enemies despite, or rather because of, his great services to the state, was yet not prepared to defend his position by subverting the whole aristocratic way of politics. He bowed to the storm and went into exile. Yet, not much more than thirty years later we have documented in the events of the Spanish wars clear evidence of a profound change in attitude.[66] It is not, primarily, that the Roman armies were constantly defeated in these wars, not that the noble commanders were incompetent, oppressive and treacherous, not even that the Senate as a body was unable to impose its will on the individual generals. It is that for the first occasion in Roman history over an extended period of time the military needs of Rome and the demands of the provinces were consistently subordinated by all sections of the nobility to factional self-interest. That one faction should attempt to turn a difficult situation to its own advantage would have been merely traditional. What was new and portentous about the Spanish wars was that the nobility as a whole treated affairs in Spain not on their merits but as they advanced their own cause and glory and retarded and diminished those of their enemies in the narrow arena of political life at Rome. It is not the least of the melancholy attractions of the study of the decline of the Roman Republic to observe how as Rome's power and empire grew everything became more and more subordinated to the factional struggles of the ruling oligarchy. Before the wars in Spain were over, the mould of second-century politics was shattered when a powerful faction of the nobility which included the leader of the Senate, Ap. Claudius Pulcher, and the tribune Ti. Sempronius Gracchus attempted to exploit Rome's difficulties to upset the political balance in their own favour. Chief among Rome's difficulties in the second century had been that of finding sufficient recruits for the army. Marius, when he ignored the property qualification in raising his troops for the Jugurthine war, solved the problem. He looked to win by his own efforts and by the political influence of his grateful veterans the prestige which far-flung hereditary *clientelae* conferred on the nobles and a position in the Senate commensurate with his achievements. The senatorial oligarchy, animated by the implacably hostile Caecilii Metelli, saw only an over-powerful outsider who had to be cut down to size. Hence the refusal to co-operate in settling the veterans of the Jugurthine and Cimbric wars, for if Marius were unable to redeem his promises by rewarding his discharged veterans, his clients, then his following based on these clients could be expected to melt away. The result, however, was Marius' uneasy alliance with Saturninus and the Senate's loss of control over the new type of army. For in the Social war, which was provoked by the persistent refusal of Roman politicians to treat the Italians and their claims as anything but pawns in the factional struggles of the capital, the soldiers became accustomed to civil war on Italian soil and to fighting not for their country against a recognizable foreign enemy but at the command of their generals against old comrades in arms. The developing professional army changed inevitably into a client army attached to its commander. The Social war gave two men at least the opportunity to realize the political possibilities of the new development: Cn. Pompeius Strabo and L. Cornelius Sulla. It was the latter who crowned the process by his treasonable compact with Mithridates and his invasion of Italy against the lawful government of Rome.[67] To secure personal position and power, to assert one's own *dignitas* any degree of force or fraud became legitimate. Catiline and Caesar document the ruin of the Republic. Catiline raised his revolution in the hope of preserving the remnants of his *dignitas*, because despite his efforts he had not received the position due to his *dignitas* and saw unworthy men preferred to him.[68] The assertion and defence of his *dignitas* was ever Caesar's ruling passion. It was for this that he formed the alliance with Pompey and Crassus known as the First Triumvirate. The ancient authorities agreed that the motive behind this compact was *potentia* and *dignitas*.[69] After the death of Crassus Caesar and Pompey faced each other, each suspicious of the other and jealous of his own *dignitas*.[70] The civil war was, from one aspect, a struggle for *dignitas*, for Caesar could not bear a superior nor Pompey an equal.[71] It was in defence of his *dignitas*, which he claimed to regard as more important than his life, that Caesar crossed the Rubicon and marched on Rome.[72] Well might Cicero exclaim 'Are we talking about a general of the Roman People or Hannibal?'[73]

The Republican tradition of *virtus* had laid it down that only by doing good to the state could a man win glory and prestige. When that tradition was shattered, when glory and prestige were sought to the detriment and destruction of the state, the Republic was destroyed, not by an external enemy, not by some abstract and inexorable process of economic or historical development, but by the ruinous lust for power and position of that very class which had traditionally identified itself most closely with the with the *respublica*—the *nobiles*.

CHAPTER III

THE NEW ORDER

'With you I experienced Philippi and swift flight, leaving my shield dishonourably behind, when virtus *was shattered and the menacing troops shamefully bit the dust.'*[1]

A SENTIMENTAL VIEW would date the death of the Republic to the defeat of Brutus and Cassius. In truth it had perished long since, before ever Caesar crossed the Rubicon. In a moment of clarity Cicero condemned both Pompey and Caesar: 'Both seek domination, both wish to rule'.[2] The formulation in Latin is important. *Regnare*, its noun *regnum* and the often associated *dominatio* are essentially terms of abuse. They were used to denote the position of a man or faction whose power and prestige had attained a predominance over those of the other *nobiles*. Thus it is said that Scipio Africanus was accused of *regnum* because of the predominance of his faction after Zama.[3] Cicero alleged that Ti. Gracchus aimed at monarchic rule (*regnum*) or rather actually reigned for a few months.[4] Similar allegations were made about Saturninus. Cinna's regime was called *dominatus* and *tyrannis*, Sulla's dictatorship *dominatio*, *tyrannis*, *regnum*.[5] Catiline's aim, we are told, was *regnum*.[6] Cicero described the land commission proposed by Rullus as a *regnum decemvirale* and was himself abused as *rex* for his suppression of Catiline's conspiracy.[7] Few, if any, of these men desired kingship as we understand it. All wished for, and some actually obtained, the power to manipulate the constitution for their own ends. *Regnum* implied loss of *libertas*, a vague term standing for a mere minimum of political rights and admitting many interpretations.[8] It became the regular form in the late Republic to accuse your opponents of *regnum* and to pose yourself as the champion of liberty, *vindex libertatis*. Thus the young Pompey raised a private army and 'liberated

Italy and the city of Rome which had been almost utterly oppressed and destroyed' from the tyranny of the Marian faction—and for the domination of Sulla.[9] Thus Caesar crossed the Rubicon 'to liberate himself and the Roman People who had been oppressed by an oligarchic faction'—and established his own *regnum*.[10] Nobody ever sought power for himself and the enslavement of others without invoking *libertas* and such fair names.[11] The freedom and liberty of the ordinary Roman were not, we may suspect, seriously impaired under a *regnum* or a *dominatio*. The only people who could claim such impairment were the political opponents of the faction which was at the moment in the enjoyment of power. For them and for their propaganda *libertas* had a peculiarly restricted sense. It stood for nothing more than the freedom to engage in the normal traffic of office and power, to manipulate the constitution to their own ends, to govern the Roman world according to their own desires and for their own profit. Caesar's *regnum*, hostile to *virtus*, impaired *libertas*. But the only liberty he impaired was that of his fellow nobles to amass prestige and power. Caesar was not concerned to disguise the fact. He paraded his *clementia*.[12] Mercy is a blessed virtue: not so the Latin concept. On the contrary, it was sharp and hostile. The true nature of Caesar's *clementia* appears clearly in Cicero's speeches for Marcellus and Ligarius, delivered in 46 BC. On Caesar's *clementia* alone depended the life of everyone and Cicero's hopes for a better future.[13] He and Ligarius were suppliants prostrate at Caesar's feet.[14] *Clementia*, in fact, denoted the arbitrary mercy, bound by no law, shown by a superior to an inferior who is entirely in his power. It is the quality proper to the *rex*.[15] In the free Republic there was no place for *rex* or *regnum*. The only body which could properly show *clementia* was the Roman People itself in its historic rôle of pardoning the humbled. The significance of Caesar's *clementia* did not escape those who, like the son of Ahenobarbus, refused to accept it. There is a certain consistency in Caesar who crowned a career spent in the assertion of his *dignitas* by crossing the Rubicon in its defence, who ended the civil war by his *clementia*, who was killed for his *regnum*. His murderers, variously motivated and variously fortified for their task, were agreed on this: Caesar's position was a negation of the Republic and what they called liberty. They acted to restore to the *nobiles* the licence to scramble for power and office. M. Iunius Brutus was the author of a book on *virtus*. While the few ancient references to the work stress its philosophic content, it had always been the tendency at Rome for philosophy to serve politics.[16] Brutus may have been concerned not with ethical abstractions, but with the political realities of glory and prestige, power and the Republic, with yet another representation and assertion of the moral and political tradition of the Roman nobility.[17] Chance has preserved for us a clear statement of his position: 'It is better', he said, 'to be master of no one than a slave to anyone. Without mastery it is possible to live honourably; with servitude life is utterly impossible.'[18] For the Roman noble the obligation to pursue the power to command was peremptory. But better far the renunciation even of this than to be prevented and thwarted by a stronger. That was not liberty and the Republic but servitude and a living death. If monarchy was to be the price of empire, better to lose the empire. Lucan's Cato put the death of genuine liberty in the time of Marius and Sulla. It was not a rash or unsupportable view.[19]

Caesar's murderers had not yet learnt that their style of politics was out of date. The Ides of March was followed not by the rebirth of the Republic and a resurgence of liberty but by chaos and proscription, civil war and a new line of monarchic faction leaders until Octavian entered into the fullness of his inheritance from Caesar and became the ruler of the world. One *princeps* displaced the *principes*, so the transition to the imperial monarchy has been defined. The formulation illuminates if we also observe that the change in number inexorably imposed a change in kind. A multiplicity of *principes*, that precisely to the *nobiles* was the free Republic. After Actium the chief, the most urgent of all Octavian's problems was to ensure that he did not suffer the fate of Caesar. Octavian's relations with the *nobiles* form a fascinating story.[20] Arriving relatively late on the Roman scene after Caesar's death Octavian seemed to the *nobiles*, who, imagining that real power had once more been restored to them, had already made their dispositions, a young nonentity to be used and discarded.[21] In his implacably ruthless rise to power his earliest associates and closest allies were men from families totally unknown before, men like Q. Salvidienus Rufus and the grim M. Vipsanius Agrippa.[22] A long time passed before any number of senators could be found on his side.[23] The turning-point came with Octavian's marriage, on 17 January 38 BC, to Livia Drusilla, a transaction of mutual profit. Livia's father, a Claudius by birth, was connected through his adoption by M. Livius Drusus, the tribune of 91 BC, with that mysterious faction from which the Optimates of the last age of the Republic in part derived. Octavian then began to attract ambitious aristocrats. They joined him not from sentiment but because they judged that he might become the equal, even the superior of Antony and carry them to power.[24] So long as Octavian was successful they would support him. Paradoxically, the greatest danger would come with peace and victory over Antony. It was then that the *nobiles* might decide to restore the Republic and their own power by removing Octavian. The *nobiles* were Augustus' natural enemies. He never trusted them.

A cynical view sees in Augustus' restoration of the Republic a hollow pretence. If the definition that the *nobiles* had imposed on the *respublica* be accepted, it was, in the sense that the real power was to remain with Augustus. This was demanded no less by the realities of the situation than the interests of the Princeps. Only the person and power of Augustus stood between Rome and the return of the chaos of factional politics and civil war. The Roman People saw this well enough. They wanted Augustus to assume more power, not less, and to assume it more openly. His renunciation of the annual consulship in the settlement of 23 BC provoked violent riots. Augustus was pressed to accept a dictatorship or a perpetual and annual consulship. After he had left for the East, the People insisted on electing him consul for 21 BC. When he refused to accept the office, they refused to elect another to fill the vacancy. It was not until Agrippa was sent to Italy in the year 21 itself that a second consul was elected. Agrippa also arranged the consular elections for the next year but after his departure the People once more at the elections for 19 insisted on reserving one consulship for Augustus. In the end the situation grew so serious that only the return of Augustus himself restored order. Spontaneous demonstrations of popular enthusiasm for any regime are rightly suspect in any age. But the agitation would scarcely have been so sustained had it not been founded on genuine popular sentiment. The People wanted security and order, not the chaos of the late Republic.[25] The desire was unlikely to have been confined to the city of Rome. To the peoples of Italy, however great their sentimental regard for the idea of the Republic, the rule of the *nobiles* had brought neglect and deceit, civil war and devastation, to the provinces overseas negligence and the perversion of their interests, exploitation and the plunder of their resources. The only section of society that could expect to benefit from the restoration of the Republic as it had lately existed were the *nobiles* themselves—and they, who had known the reality, were not to be taken in by any sham.

The concept *respublica* shared the essential vagueness common to all Roman political thought.[26] Just as *libertas* denoted a bare minimum of political rights, so *respublica* denoted a bare minimum of political organization: the magistrates, the Senate, the assemblies of the Roman People. Beyond this its concrete content was small. It said little or nothing of the balance of power between the three basic constituents of the Republican constitution. During what both we and the Romans termed the free Republic the balance of power had shifted many times, from the magistrates to the People, from the People to the Senate, from the Senate to the People again. And throughout none of these organs had actually ruled but an oligarchy had ruled through them. Indeed, the whole notion of a 'Republican constitution' is anachronistic and misleading. As the Greek political thinkers saw, it did not exist. What did exist was the chaotic result of a series of *ad hoc* concessions to forestall internal revolution mingled with archaic survivals and preserved by an excessive conservatism to produce a number of ill-defined, overlapping and potentially conflicting sources of power and authority. *Respublica* was less an intellectual concept than an emotion, less a description of a specific form of government than a pledge of a purpose of government.[27] It stood above all for the rule of law and the assurance of the rights and liberties of the Roman People. History can show few politicians equal to Augustus and none his superior. In admiring contemplation of his political craft we may neglect to observe that he was a Roman and that his mind moved in Roman categories. This, if anything, is demonstrated by the *Res Gestae*, in what that document includes and in what it omits and, above all, in its astonishing opening: 'At the age of nineteen I raised an army on my own initiative and at my own expense and with it I liberated the Republic which was oppressed by the domination of a faction.'[28] It is the traditional Roman justification for armed usurpation. There is no reason to suspect Augustus of irony. The re-establishment of legitimate government, the restoration of the rule of law, the reaffirmation of the rights and liberties of the citizens—there was only one phrase in Latin, hallowed by traditional usage, to comprehend all this: *respublica restituta*. The harsh condemnation of Augustus' restoration of the Republic as fraudulent is erroneous because it supposes that the Latin term denoted primarily a specific structure of government and a specific distribution of power. Augustus restored the Republic in the same sense, though not in the same form, as Sulla re-established it. The concept was elastic enough to admit both interpretations and many others. There was no fraud; no one was deceived. Augustus announced not primarily nor most importantly the restoration of a specific form of government, beyond the irreducible minimum that the traditional institutions would continue to exist, but precisely that the lawless anarchy of the past years was ended, that military usurpation and the rule of force had given way to legitimate government and the rule of law. It was, if you like, an act of self-legitimization. But if Augustus had *not* 'restored the Republic', then there would have been cause for wonder and debate. Not to restore the Republic probably never entered Augustus' head, though the exact form of the restoration was the product of anxious deliberation. The military dynasts of the first century BC, Sulla and Octavian, Pompey and Caesar, were the most conservative of revolutionaries. The long revolution which culminated in the establishment of the Principate was an accidental by-product of the satisfaction of personal ambition. Essentially there was no difference between the dynasts and the rest of the *nobiles*. They were more ruthless and more successful, that is all. But in the process the Roman state was transformed. Velleius Paterculus referred to the Augustan settlement as 'the recall of the original and ancient form of the Republic'; Suetonius wrote of the creation of a 'new order'.[29] Both, in a sense, were right. Traditional rights and liberties, virtues and standards were to be safeguarded by a new political dispensation which had developed from the old: this was what was announced on 13 January 27 BC. Augustan propaganda insisted on continuity with the past, rightly. What had happened was that the notion of the *respublica*, with the easy malleability characteristic of all Roman political ideas, had reached a further stage of development.

The new order, replacing the self-seeking chaos that had gone before, required a new ideal. At first sight, Virgil's treatment of the concept of *virtus* in the *Aeneid* seems thoroughly traditional. The majority of occurrences of the word are in military contexts.[30] Such expressions are conventional in Latin literature of all ages. While 'bravery' or 'courage' may offer themselves as convenient translations, the Latin implied something more: manliness in the service of the state by the performance of exemplary deeds according to proper standards of conduct. Similarly the conventional phrase for the award of Roman citizenship, *virtutis causa*, implies not merely nor necessarily bravery, but meritorious service to the Roman state. With *virtus* Virgil contrasts luck and fortune, deceit and trickery.[31] Basically *virtus* consists in winning by one's deeds an undying fame which will live on after the body is dead: 'There stands for each man his appointed day; short and irrevocable is the period of man's life; but to stretch out fame by deeds, that is the task of *virtus*'.[32] Fame and honour are the rewards of *virtus* and, conversely, it is *virtus* to seek them by brave deeds.[33] Since *virtus* is attained and increased by personal deeds, both it and the fame won by it are personal. *Virtus* is not inherited. Ancestors are important only for the standards they set and as examples to excite emulation.[34] But by one's own labours one can equal and surpass one's ancestors and even aspire to join the gods.[35] All this, through briefly stated, can be seen to lie well within the lines of development we have already traced.

But, conventional, even traditional, though this may appear, there is one important omission. In the Republican tradition, *nobilis* and *novus*, though bitterly divided over the claims of birth, were yet in firm agreement as to the ends and aims of *virtus*. From the Scipionic epitaphs, Plautus and Ennius to Cicero and Sallust we meet incessant insistence that what was sought by *virtus* was not merely a general and promiscuous reputation, but, specifically, *gloria*, to which the tradition gave a hard and definite connotation.[36] Once and once only did Virgil bring *virtus* and *gloria* together: 'I, Turnus, second to none of the men of old in *virtus*, have vowed this my life to you and to Latinus, the father of my bride. "Aeneas challenges to single combat." I pray that he would challenge. Nor should Drances, if this is the anger of the gods, pay with his death, nor, if it is *virtus* and *gloria*, should he carry them off.'[37] Here, as rarely in the *Aeneid*, speaks the authentic voice of the ideal Roman aristocrat as we meet him in the Scipionic epitaphs, in Ennius and in Livy. And it speaks through the mouth not of Aeneas or any of the Trojans but of the leader of Italian resistance to them and to the foundation of Rome. Turnus' devotion to his people, his claim of pre-eminence not merely among his contemporaries but among the men of old, his assertion of his right to the rewards of *virtus* and *gloria* all belong to the Roman tradition. Turnus occupies a vital place in the economy of the *Aeneid*, which it is impossible to analyse here in all its aspects.[38] He is no monster. Young and the most handsome of the Italians, he combines royal ancestry and personal achievement.[39] Patriotic, he fights for Italy and to expel the foreign invaders and he combines patriotism with piety.[40] Yet, for all his virtues, Turnus is a disruptive force. His *virtus* is wild and untamed, *ferox*, as king Latinus sees.[41] Virgil himself presses the point home in the similes which characterize Turnus: he is like a wild beast.[42] Above all, he is *superbus*. As used by Virgil this adjective covers a wide range of meaning. At the one extreme it denotes splendour or an exulting pride in achievement.[43] At the other, it stands for the cruel and overweening arrogance of the king and tyrant which destroys justice and reduces men to slavery.[44] Turnus' natural pride in his birth and station, his humanity and his piety turn to arrogance. He becomes a tyrant.[45] Such men are an affront to justice and civilized society. It is Rome's duty, ordained by heaven, in imposing peace to destroy them in war.[46]

Turnus fights for Italy. But the whole theme of the *Aeneid* is the foundation struggle not of a single city but of a unified nation. 'So great a task was it to found the Roman race'.[47] The last word in the line is as important as its beginning. Rome was to exist not merely as a city built with hands but as a natural entity. And this entity, for Virgil, was to arise from a union with Italy in which *Itala virtus* was to give strength to Rome.[48] Speaking easily and naturally of Italy we are not always aware how slowly the notion developed that the multiplicity of nations and tribes who inhabited the Italian peninsula had a community of interest which united them against the rest of the world. The first glimmerings of the idea arose from the external threat posed by the Gauls and by Pyrrhus. But the expansion of Roman power and the ravages of Hannibal were as much divisive as cohesive. The real impetus came only with the Roman nobility's deliberate subordination of the Italian demand for citizenship to their own temporary advantage. In the Social war, *Italia* was the name of the rebel confederacy. In the propaganda campaign before Actium Octavian had appealed to the *consensus Italiae*. The battle of Actium was separated from the revolt of the Italian allies by a mere sixty years. It was not the least of the achievements of Augustus that under him the unity of Italy moved from an imperfectly formulated aspiration or a propaganda fraud to solid and enduring reality. It was this unity that Turnus obstructed. His cause may have been noble, but it was the wrong one.

Gloria in the late Republic had been intimately connected not merely with the concept of *virtus* but with *nobilitas*. The word *nobilitas* is found only once in the *Aeneid* and that, precisely, is in the same episode as Turnus' association of *virtus* and *gloria*. Turnus' solemn assertion of his *virtus* and devotion to his cause was provoked by the attack of Drances 'hostile to Turnus whose *gloria* stirred him with the bitter goads of underhand envy, a man open with his wealth and better than most with his tongue, but impotent in war, a man considered a weighty instigator of policy, powerful in political faction (nobility inherited from his mother gave him arrogance of race, the standing of his father was unknown)'.[49] It might almost be an hostile portrait of a late Republican politician. Virgil, more than any other poet, wrote with perfect mastery of his material and medium. It can be no accident that from his concept of *virtus* he dropped precisely those ideas, *gloria* and *nobilitas*, which had featured most prominently in the preceding age. Nor can it be accidental that the only time that *virtus*, *gloria* and *nobilitas* do occur together in the *Aeneid* it is in connection with Turnus. Turnus (and Drances too) was an anachronism. His ferocious *virtus*, his *gloria* were as much outdated as the separate Italy he defended. Virgil's attitude was consistent. Three times members of Aeneas' force act in defence or pursuit of individual *gloria*; on all three occasions the attempt ends in disaster. Entellus is overtaken by homicidal mania; Euryalus and Pallas go to their deaths.[50] The assertion of individual *gloria* was always, for Virgil, divisive and destructive. True *gloria* attended the foundation of a secure society based not merely on war but on the rule of law and extending its civilizing influence over the whole world.[51] Aeneas, though amply qualified by his honourable birth and his fame which had mounted to heaven, lacks, precisely and deliberately, *gloria* and *nobilitas*. His great quality, emphasized and invoked at every turn of the poem, is *pietas*. It means nothing else than doing his duty to his gods, his country and his family.[52] This duty Aeneas pursues against his own will, in violation of his passionate desire for rest and tranquillity, with growing steadfastness and deepening understanding of his destiny. Early in the poem he is characterized: 'Our king was Aeneas, than whom none was more just or greater in dutifulness and war.'[53] *Pietas* went hand in hand with *iustitia*.[54] *Pietas* left no room for the assertion of personal glory; by *iustitia* the *superbi* were tamed and made into a civilized nation.[55]

The traditional aristocratic concept of *virtus* prescribed winning glory in the service of the state. The *nobiles* of the late Republic by pursuing *gloria* at the expense of the state had destroyed the *respublica*. Virgil redressed the balance. All that the *nobiles* had meant by *gloria* he showed to be false and disruptive. Devotion to Rome and to Rome's mission was the test of *virtus*. 'I am dutiful Aeneas'—it is a far cry from the ruinous self-assertion of the *nobiles*. As a foil to the revolutionary Catiline, Virgil chose Cato and pictured him engaged, precisely, in administering law and justice among the blessed dead.[56] Even the cantankerous Sallust, no friend to the fraud of politicians, had praised Cato for his integrity and severity, his steadfastness and self-control, his probity and his temperance.[57] And between Catiline and Cato Virgil placed Augustus himself, the visible symbol of national unity, 'leading into battle the Italians with the senators and the People and the gods of the home and state'.[58]

Virgil, it is important to observe, did not stand alone in this attitude. *Gloria* occurs but seldom in the poems of Horace. Although the connection with warfare and politics is maintained,[59] *gloria*, apart from one jokingly erotic allusion to military glory,[60] is consistently represented as something detrimental. '*Gloria* that lifts its empty head too high' has as its natural companions blind love of self and faith that betrays its secrets.[61] *Gloria* rides in a shining chariot and drags as its prisoners bound hand and foot both noble and humble.[62] *Gloria* ruins a man like an insatiable appetite for sex, gambling or money.[63] 'That *gloria* shall not attract you, I will bind you both by an oath: whichever of you becomes aedile or praetor, let him be disinherited and accursed.'[64] *Fama*, *decus* and *honos* all stand in a good sense; but not *gloria*, which had the most specific connotation of all. *Dulce et decorum est pro patria mori* is arguably the most famous line that Horace wrote: the Republican tradition would, like Virgil's Turnus, inevitably have invoked *gloria*.[65]

Gloria, for Horace, was no part of *virtus*; neither was *nobilitas*. The noun, indeed, is not found in Horace's works. That is scarcely surprising: it was a clumsy and unpoetic word. The adjective *nobilis*, however, is not uncommon. But in over half the instances it reverts to its basic meaning of 'well-known' whether generally or for some specific quality or achievement.[66] In this sense it is applied to persons such as Sybaris, who was *nobilis* for having hurled the discus or the javelin beyond the mark, or the sons of Leda, one *nobilis* for victories with horses, the other for winning at boxing; to places such as the fountain of Bandusia, Luceria and Crete; to the Trojan war; to the books of the philosopher Panaetius and to the trimeters of the poet Accius. *Nobilitas* is thus connected with great achievement and fame. It is also connected with birth.[67] But of the specifically political sense there is barely a trace: a certain Vergilius, not the poet, is described as 'a client of noble youths'; Paullus Fabius Maximus is termed *nobilis* (it could hardly have been avoided) as is Aelius Lamia 'descended from Lamus of old, since from him they say that the Lamiae of earlier times were named and the whole race of their descendants through the recording fasti'.[68] Something of this sense seems to reside in an extended political image in which Horace explodes with indignation at the poor reception given to his *Odes*: 'I do not buy the votes of the fickle mob with the expense of dinners and the gift of out-worn clothes; I, the disciple and avenger of the noble poets, do not deign to canvass the tribes of the grammarians and their platforms.'[69] *Nobilitas* denoted a certain status and might form the occasion for a graceful compliment similar to the references to Maecenas' royal ancestry. But real quality resided elsewhere. Pride in race and name may turn out to be an empty boast: painted sterns do not necessarily make sound ships.[70]

As in Virgil's *Aeneid*, so in the poems of Horace *gloria* and *nobilitas* are dissociated from *virtus*. *Virtus* is a frequent topic in Horace's works. We may here leave on one side such philosophic tags as '*Virtus* is the mean of vices and removed from both extremes' and such expressions as 'therefore it is not enough to draw a grin from your hearer—though even that is a certain *virtus*'.[71] *Virtus*, in the sense with which we are concerned, meant, for Horace, acting in a manly fashion. The man of *virtus* sought the great rewards of his merits. 'Either *virtus* is an empty word or the man who tries rightly aims at honour and reward'.[72] Honour is achieved by great deeds, as in the case of Ulysses whom Homer 'set before us as a useful example of the power of *virtus* and wisdom'. He tamed Troy and endured many hardships on his return to Greece, but was never overwhelmed by the waves of adversity.[73] *Virtus* and honour do not attend sloth; only what is won by *virtus* is truly praiseworthy.[74] For *virtus* implies a proper standard of conduct: mere achievement, however great, is not enough. Therefore we find *virtus* associated with such moral qualities as frugality, agreeability, simplicity and courage; honesty and modesty; good sense and prudence.[75] It was a constant tradition at Rome to preach moral standards by exemplifying now the noble savage, now the Romans of an earlier age, now the rustic virtue of the remote parts of Italy. Thus Horace contrasts the contemporary Romans who 'enviously hate *virtus* while it is safe and seek it when it is lost' and who have left 'the steep path of *virtus*' now with the unbending Getae among whom orphans were cared for by other women, where a man was master in his own house and all wives were faithful, who looked to the great *virtus* of their parents as their dowry, who regarded sin as a curse and the penalty for it death; now with those Romans who had conquered Pyrrhus and the Carthaginians, Hannibal and Antiochus and who were the sons of peasant soldiers trained in the hard school of farming in the Sabine country and obedience to a strict mother; now with the innocent pleasures and difficult toil of country life far from Rome, the forum and arrogant politicians.[76] Both the great deeds and the moral qualities by which fame and honour are won Horace terms *virtutes* as being the objective expressions of *virtus*.[77] All this, with the one important exception of the omission of *gloria*, is, of course, thoroughly traditional, as is implied by the heroes to whom *virtus* is attributed: Anchises and the descendants of Venus, Regulus, the two Africani and, above all, Cato the Censor and his descendant, Caesar's great enemy.[78] Traditional too is the concentration on *virtus* in public life, in peace and war, opposed to the teachings of philosophy: 'At one time I become a man of action and drown myself in the waves of public life as the guardian and unbending follower of true *virtus*; at another I slip back furtively into the teachings of Aristippus and try to submit circumstances to myself, not myself to circumstances.'[79] True *virtus* consists in the unremitting and impartial administration of the affairs of state, which earns the highest honour: '*Virtus*, ignorant of sordid defeat, shines with unsullied honours nor does it take up or lay down the axes of power at the whim of the fickle mob. *Virtus*, opening heaven for those who deserve not to die, attempts its journey by a way denied to others and despises the common herd and the damp earth on flying wings.'[80] The greatest honour is that of Augustus himself: 'What care on the part of the senators and the Roman People, Augustus, will immortalize forever with full gifts of honours your *virtutes* by inscriptions and the recording fasti.' But while warfare is glorious, the arts of peace raise men to heaven. Addressing Augustus who 'alone bears the weight of all public affairs, guards the state of Italy in war, adorns her with morals, reforms her with laws' Horace recounts the enormous deeds (*ingentia facta*) of Romulus, father Liber, Castor and Pollux who after death were received among the gods: in life they cared for the land and the race of men, settled fierce wars, assigned lands and founded towns.[81]

Virtus had nothing to do with birth or antiquity of pedigree. Horace attacks the man 'who betakes himself to the fasti and values *virtus* by years and admires only what Libitina, the goddess of funerals, has sanctified'.[82] Indeed birth and *virtus* are opposed: 'You will say that I, born a freedman's son in humble circumstances, spread my wings too wide for my nest (thus you will add to my *virtus* as much as you take from my birth) and that in peace and war I pleased the leaders of the state.'[83] This accords with Horace's attitude to *nobilitas*. He agreed with the new men of the late Republic who attacked as a perversion of the ideal the nobles' claim that *virtus* could be inherited.[84] Yet on one occasion he reproduced the view of the *nobiles* in all its extremity: 'From the brave and good the brave are born; there is in steers and horses the *virtus* of their fathers; fierce eagles do not beget unwarlike doves.'[85] The explanation of this startling departure is to be found in the subject of the poem. It is an ode in honour of the Alpine victories of Drusus. Drusus was a Claudius, the son of Livia Drusilla and Ti. Claudius Nero. Throughout Roman history the Claudii had distinguished themselves by their relentless insistence on the privileges and prerogatives of aristocratic birth: their enemies had called it *superbia*, tyrannical arrogance. Horace here insisted on Drusus' family and its services to Rome. But, even more than a Claudius, Drusus was the stepson of Augustus. Here we approach the real significance of the Principate. It was not so much that Augustus, as is sufficiently shown by his unceasing but unsuccessful attempts to find an heir in his own blood, had all the pride of family typical of a Roman aristocrat. It was that when one *princeps* displaced the *principes*, he inevitably concentrated on himself all the privileges and prerogatives which they had shared and for which they had struggled. All real power and position, *auctoritas*, *dignitas* and *gloria*, had passed into the possession of one man. Militarily it was Augustus who held the *auspicia* and it was he who was the commander of the Roman army in his wide *provincia*. Therefore it was he alone who was entitled to celebrate a triumph.[86] Only to Augustus could the aristocratic concept of *virtus* be applied in all its fullness; only to members of his family might a share be granted—and even they benefited from his teaching and example.[87]

The agreement of Horace and Virgil in dethroning *gloria* from its previous eminence in the concept of *virtus* and in dissociating this concept from the idea of *nobilitas* cannot be accidental. There was no room in the new order for the pursuit of the *gloria* which had ruined the Republic. 'Faith and Peace and Honour and ancient Modesty and neglected *Virtus* dare to return and blessed Plenty with her full horn appears.'[88] The establishment of peace and security in Rome and Rome's empire, this was the task of *virtus*. Like Aeneas the politicians of the new Republic were not to be heroes in the vulgar sense: the world had suffered enough from such heroics. Civil war, the devastation of Italy, the plundering of the provinces—this is what the pursuit of *gloria* and the assertion of the claims of *nobilitas* had meant. Aeneas' aim was not personal domination but to unify and reconcile

Rome and Italy on the basis of law, not conquest.[89] Again and again Horace insisted that it was Augustus who had saved the Roman world from ruin and that it was Augustus alone who prevented the return of chaos: 'I will fear neither civil war nor violent death while Caesar rules the earth.'[90] In the last of his *Odes*, perhaps the last of all his poems, Horace reviewed the blessings of Augustus' rule: 'While Caesar guards affairs civil madness or violence will not banish peace nor will anger which forges swords and threatens wretched cities. Those who drink the deep Danube shall not break the Julian edicts, nor the Getae, nor the Seres or the faithless Parthians, nor those born by the river Tanais.'[91] You may call it propaganda if you wish. But Virgil and Horace were not hypocrites—and they were right. It was not Augustus nor any of the other monarchic faction leaders who remarked that civil war was worse than monarchy: it was M. Favonius, the fanatical adherent of Caesar's enemy, Cato.[92] The propaganda of Augustus succeeded precisely because, unlike the polemic of the factional strife of the last age of the Republic, it was founded ultimately on real issues. Before Actium, the consensus of Italy was a real aspiration, on which Horace agreed with Virgil, and the division of the Roman world into West and East corresponded to a real fear.[93] After the 'restoration of the Republic', order, security and the *Pax Augusta* answered men's prayers. For them the free Republic was well lost. It is dangerously easy to take the Republican *nobiles* at their own valuation.

In strong contrast to Virgil and Horace is the historian Livy. His work, as we have it, is a celebration of *virtus Romana* in the individual and the state. As R. S. Conway put it, 'it is to Livy more than any other writer that we owe our conception of the Roman national character'. At the very beginning of the *History* Romulus defines the two factors which have established Rome and will establish her empire: the favour of the gods and the *virtus* of the city and its citizens.[94] By *virtus* Livy meant the conventional ideal of the Republican aristocracy: the winning of *gloria* and personal pre-eminence by the meritorious service of the state. Thus C. Mucius, failing in his attempt to assassinate Lars Porsenna, claimed 'to do and to suffer bravely is the Roman way' and proceeded to prove his point by burning off his right hand with the remark 'look and see how cheap the body is to those who behold great *gloria*'. Porsenna agreed with Mucius: 'I would say "well done", if that *virtus* of yours were at the disposal of my country.' Both he and the Romans accorded Mucius the honour which was the natural due of *virtus*.[95] Such displays of *virtus* not only won pre-eminent glory for the individual but also, traditionally, excited others to emulation. Thus Mucius inspired Cloelia, though a woman, to demonstrate her *virtus*: a new kind of manliness which the Roman state, appropriately, accorded a new kind of honour.[96] Again, of Kaeso Quinctius 'T. Quinctius Capitolinus, who had been thrice consul, after he had referred to the many honours which he himself and his family had won, declared that neither in the clan of the Quinctii nor in the Roman state had there ever existed so great a nature of such ripe *virtus*; Kaeso had served his first campaigns under his command and had, in his own frequent sight, fought against the enemy. Sp. Furius said that Kaeso, sent by Quinctius Capitolinus, had arrived to relieve him when he had got into difficulties: Kaeso had done more than any one man, in Furius' estimation, to restore the situation. L. Lucretius, the consul of the previous year, shining with *gloria* still fresh, said that the praise he had won belonged to Kaeso as well. He recounted Kaeso's battles and mentioned his outstanding deeds both on expeditions and in the battle-line. He urged and advised that the outstanding young man, equipped with all the advantages of nature and fortune, would have the greatest effect on public affairs in whatever state he went to. The Romans should prefer him to be a citizen of Rome than of another state.'[97] *Virtus*, we see, consisted in the employment of one's natural gifts to the full to perform outstanding deeds which, in turn, brought *gloria* in the specific form of recognition by the leading men of one's family and class. Again, the murder of Sp. Maelius by C. Servilius Ahala was approved as an act of *virtus*, not 'courage', since Maelius was unarmed and in terrified flight, but the commission of an exemplary deed in the service of Rome. Maelius was represented as aiming at kingship; Servilius had liberated the state; the preservation of the *respublica* was the highest form of *virtus*.[98] To move from legendary to historical times, though not necessarily from fiction to fact, 'although the rest at large received the news with joy and great *gloria*, P. Cornelius Scipio alone, who had achieved it, insatiable for *virtus* and true praise, regarded the recovery of the Spains as a small thing compared with what he conceived in hope and greatness of spirit. Already he looked to Africa and great Carthage and the *gloria* of that war as though it were consummated in his own honour and fame.'[99] Given the nature of Roman history and Roman historiography it is *gloria* in war and military *virtus* that predominate in Livy's work. But the arts of peace, no less than those of war, gave room for the exercise of *virtus* and the acquisition of *gloria*, less spectacular perhaps, but none the less real when tested by the standard of the preservation of the state.[100]

Virtus also demanded adherence to certain standards of conduct. Thus it was characteristic of Tarquinius Superbus that he attacked the town of Gabii 'by a method supremely un-Roman, by fraud and guile'.[101] On the other hand, Camillus rejected a victory offered him by a trick with the words 'war no less than peace has its rules and we have learnt to wage both with justice no less than with courage. . . . I will conquer by Roman methods, by *virtus*, by labour and by arms.' Sharp practice against Perseus by Q. Marcius Philippus and by A. Atilius Serranus was criticized by certain senators: 'It was not by ambushes and night raids, not by pretended flight followed by sudden attacks on the enemy who had been thrown off his guard, not with pride in trickery rather than in true glory that our ancestors waged war.' This, the senators concluded in disapproval, was a 'new and over-clever wisdom'. They, mindful of the old ways, regretted the passing of the days of high principle when the Senate turned over a potential poisoner to Pyrrhus and always declared war before waging it.[102] The rules of peace and war were few, simple and traditional. Chief among them was *fides*, good faith and the obligation to observe promises solemnly made, whether between individuals or between states, and *pietas*, especially in the sense of the observance of duty towards the gods. The two qualities interacted. Camillus by observing the demands of *fides* and justice won a bloodless victory.[103] Through neglect of the gods and of the laws C. Flaminius lost an army at Lake Trasimene.[104] The character of Hannibal, although he, like Sallust's Catiline, possessed some of the physical and mental qualifications for *virtus*, was vitiated by 'inhuman cruelty, perfidy even greater than normal in a Carthaginian, utter lack of respect for the truth, the sacred, the gods, no reverence for oaths, no religious scruple'.[105] Livy was, of course, committed to the typically Roman view of history which saw political, social and economic change in terms of morals. In his preface he spoke of vice and a decline in morality and remarked that no state had fallen to avarice and luxury so late or had honoured poverty and thrift so much or so long. 'Desire was lacking in proportion to the lack of means; recently riches have brought avarice and abounding pleasures the longing to ruin and lose everything through luxury and lust.'[106] Thus the monarchy fell because of the cruel arrogance and lust of the regal family. Peace, Livy repeated incessantly in the early books, brought luxury, moral decline and, thence, political discord. World empire and contact with foreign peoples sowed the seeds of future luxury which destroyed the old Roman way of life.

Livy was a traditionalist. The nobles of the late Republic had claimed that birth was an essential part of *virtus*: their opponents had put forward the opposing view that nobility was founded only on personal achievements. To Livy both birth and deeds deserved praise.[107] On the one hand, nobility of birth was a gift from the gods comparable to bodily strength.[108] On the other, the tribune Canuleius urged with full force the case of the *novi homines*: 'Thus, while no one despised the birth of a man in whom *virtus* shone forth, the Roman power grew. Should you be ashamed of a plebeian as consul, when our ancestors did not despise foreigners as kings and even after the expulsion of the kings the city was not closed to foreign *virtus*? . . . . Do we believe that it is impossible that a plebeian should be a brave and active man, good in peace and war like Numa, L. Tarquinius, Ser. Tullius, or that even if he is we should not allow him to undertake the government of the state? Shall we rather have as consuls men like the decemvirs, the foulest of creatures, who were all Patricians, than men like the best of the kings, new men?'[109] In the case of the Etruscan Lucumo, the later L. Tarquinius Priscus, the two views of nobility were reconciled. His wife Tanaquil urged that 'in a new people, where all nobility was sudden and arose from *virtus*, there would be a place for a brave and active man. Tatius the Sabine had become king, Numa had been summoned to reign from Cures and Ancus was born of a Sabine mother and noble only by the one bust of Numa.'[110] As citizenship granted to a foreigner *virtutis causa* was inherited by his descendants, so *nobilitas* won by a new man by personal *virtus* yet passed to his children. The reconciliation is Ciceronian rather than Sallustian.

By his repeated insistence on the essential connection between *virtus*, *gloria* and *nobilitas*, examples of which could be multiplied almost endlessly, Livy put himself in opposition to Virgil and Horace. Livy did not belong to the senatorial tradition of Roman historiography. He was a scholar, remote from and inexperienced in public affairs.[111] The writing of history at Rome was traditionally a political exercise undertaken by political men. Even the morose Sallust, sourly condemning all factions, yet took a political stand. He knew and made plain which concept of *virtus*, *gloria*, *nobilitas* he considered correct. Livy, on the contrary, involved with Rome, was detached from the issues of political polemic. His history was undertaken, not as a contribution to politics, but an escape alike from political remedies as from political ills. Familiar with the household of Augustus, he encouraged the young Claudius to write history.[112] Yet his detachment extended to Augustus' new order. The references to Augustus in his *History* are factual and without flattery.[113] The Princeps went out of his way to put the historian right on the facts of Cornelius Cossus' rank when he won the *spolia opima*, a matter of contemporary relevance. Livy duly recorded the information and its origin in a footnote: he did not bother to rewrite his account to conform with so high an authority.[114] Livy revealed his attitude in sundry ways, not least in his use of the word *princeps* which conveys no hint of the Augustan sense and in his assertion of the conventional aristocratic ideal against Virgil and Horace.[115] Augustus called him a Pompeian.[116] The truth was deeper than mere praise of Pompey. As we have it, Livy's *History* is a tacit lament for an ideal which the Principate had abolished.

CHAPTER IV

THE EMPEROR'S SERVANTS

'Let those whose habit it is to admire forbidden ideals know that even under bad emperors good men can exist and that obedience and self-control, when industry and energy are present, attain the same height of honour as many men have achieved by perilous courses, who have became famous by deaths ostentatious but useless to the state.'[1]

THE ESTABLISHMENT and continuance of the Principate was assured not so much by any specific act of constitutional legislation or partisan propaganda as by an accident of nature, the longevity, against all men's expectations and some men's hopes, of Augustus. When he died in AD 14 the battle of Actium was almost forty-five years in the past. No one under the age of sixty had any recollection of the dictatorship of Caesar, let alone of the free Republic. And after Augustus Tiberius reigned for twenty-three years.[2] The restoration of the Republic in the definition of the Republican nobility had long since ceased to be practical policy and rapidly declined into a display of sentimentality or affection. A new generation of administrators grew up wholly within the context of the monarchial system and identified the system's interests with their own. Their administration was approved by the only test applicable to governmental forms—it worked; and it worked, above all, in that it ensured to those living within the boundaries of the Roman empire a more efficient government and a greater degree of stability and security. The personalities of the individual emperors were, ultimately, irrelevant to the achievement of these desirable conditions. One man cannot rule an empire; one man cannot even rule a single city. Every form of government requires a body of administrators to shape policy, to apply policy to specific conditions, to carry the resulting decisions into effect. It was thanks to these men that the Roman imperial system continued to function whether the emperor was an insane juvenile delinquent, a rough and unsubtle soldier or even a philosopher. The government of Rome remained, essentially, what it had always been, oligarchic.

Virgil and Horace rejected the necessary connection of *gloria* as it had been interpreted in the late Republic with the Roman political tradition. But theirs was a personal reaction. It was scarcely possible for their reinterpretation, produced by whatever reason of personal reaction to the past events, present situation and future needs, permanently to impose itself. The desire for distinction and especially for that special form of distinction designated as *gloria* was too deep-seated a part of the consciousness and tradition of the Roman political class. Livy, as we have seen, continued in the same age as Virgil and Horace to assert the claims of political glory. In the works of Tacitus, too, we find *gloria* accepted as an integral component of the complex of ideas and aspirations summed up in the term *virtus*.

Tacitus recognized *virtus* as the peculiar attribute of the human race which distinguished it from the dumb beasts and secured the favour of the gods.[3] Within mankind, *virtus* belonged to the free man since it involved an exercise of the will and the display of qualities not open to the slave.[4] It formed, with fortune, one of the two great principles which governed human affairs. But while *virtus* was rational and certain, fortune was irrational and unpredictable. The gifts of fortune, though pleasant, even desirable, were nevertheless dangerous since they tended to corrupt and were awarded and removed without regard to merit.[5] The operation of fortune might even nullify the effects of the exercise of *virtus* and thus upset the proper order of things.[6] To represent the gratuitous benefits of capricious fortune as the achievements of *virtus* Tacitus considered fraudulent.[7]

Above all, *virtus* formed the ancestral foundation of the Roman state and attached both to the people and to the empire of Rome.[8] For men to struggle with each other over *virtus* and to compete for *gloria* was not merely natural but a mark of felicity.[9] *Virtus* demanded recognition and honour; to insist on and to strive for them was praiseworthy.[10] Specifically, *gloria* was won by the objective expression of *virtus*, by *virtutes*. Traditionally, *gloria* was as natural response to *virtutes* as repentance was to the commission of a crime.[11] Thus Agricola by his *virtutes* was carried headlong to glory and thus Tiberius could write to Sejanus 'nothing is so exalted that your *virtutes* and your devotion to me have not merited it'.[12] For himself Tiberius rejected divine honours. This, Tacitus remarked, some interpreted as modesty, many as lack of confidence, a few as the sign of a degenerate spirit. 'They argued that the best men entertained the highest desires. Thus among the Greeks Hercules and Liber, among the Romans Quirinus, had been added to the company of the gods. Augustus had behaved better: he had hoped. For emperors everything else was instantly provided: for one thing they had to work and never find satisfaction—a good reputation after death; contempt of reputation meant contempt of *virtutes*.'[13] The attitude was typically Roman: the only assurance of proper conduct lies in concern for your reputation and the man who shows himself careless of what others think of him convicts himself as careless of morality. Conversely, for *virtutes* not to receive their proper recognition was accounted scandalous. The funeral of Germanicus, although, as was fitting on such an occasion, distinguished by praise and commemoration of his *virtutes*, lacked the busts of his ancestors and the usual procession. That he was thus deprived of honours due to each and every noble was a matter of complaint at Rome. Where, men asked, were the customary practices of antiquity—the image placed before the bier, the poems designed to perpetuate the dead man's *virtus*, the eulogies and the tears, or at least the imitations of grief?[14]

Virtus expressed itself in or begot *virtutes* which commanded recognition in glory bestowed by contemporaries in life and assured after death by the proper funeral ceremonies, the recollection of posterity and commemoration in history.[15] Tacitus' position was thoroughly traditional. So too was his belief that the highest field in which *virtus* could be exercised, *virtutes* displayed and *gloria* won was the service of the state. Writing of the proposal of P. Dolabella in AD 47 that gladiatorial games should be given annually at the expense of the quaestors designate, Tacitus remarked 'among our ancestors office was the reward of *virtus* and all citizens who trusted in their good qualities were allowed to seek magistracies'.[16] The claims of *virtus* to the enjoyment of office and power had a moral content in that they were based on the good qualities of the candidates. Indeed, Tacitus elsewhere varied the time-honoured phrase to describe public offices as the rewards, not of *virtus*, but of *virtutes*.[17] *Virtutes* were the foundation of public life and action; the vices of a politician could destroy the empire.[18] *Gloria* consisted in the display and exercise of *virtutes* and the winning of public position and distinction.[19]

The notion of *virtutes*, as we have seen, had from the beginning two interrelated aspects: that of moral qualities and that of great deeds. With the latter Tacitus was not much concerned. Given that the purpose of history is to record the deeds and characters of famous men, their achievements are duly chronicled. But they are not over-stressed. Perhaps this was partly because the times and the political situation precluded outstanding deeds by the individual; but partly, we may suspect, because Tacitus had not much time for heroics of that sort. His concern is not primarily with what men did but with why they did it. He looked to motive. Consequently for him *virtutes*, as is shown by his frequent employment of the Sallustian synonym *bonae artes*, 'good practices', meant moral qualities.[20] In this category Tacitus included integrity and temperance, industry and energy, moderation and fortitude, liberality in an honourable cause and, above all, *fides*, the paramount Roman virtue.[21] At the beginning of the *Histories* Tacitus remarked that the period he was to treat was checkered by disasters, terrible with battles, torn by civil war and disgustingly cruel even in peace. Yet he found noble examples of *virtutes*: 'mothers accompanied their children in flight, wives followed their husbands into exile, relatives were brave, sons-in-law stood firm, slaves were defiantly faithful even under torture; famous men bore the last necessities courageously and their deaths equalled the famous deaths of the men of old'.[22] Again, comparing

Vespasian and Mucianus, Tacitus said that if the faults of the two men had been removed the mixture of their virtues in one man would have made a remarkably balanced combination for an emperor. Vespasian he characterized as energetic in war, a good strategist, eating whatever food offered itself, wearing a uniform little different from that of a common soldier, as comparable, in fact, to the generals of old—if he had not been avaricious. Mucianus, on the other hand, stood out by his magnificence and wealth and because in every way he lived far above the scale of a private citizen. He was a readier speaker than Vespasian and experienced both in the administration and in the formation of policy in civil affairs.[23] The examples could be greatly extended. Such being Tacitus' preoccupation, he had a keen eye for hypocrisy and fraud.[24]

Virtutes were the strength of good men, and by using them, especially in public life, *gloria* was won.[25] But although Tacitus admitted *gloria* into his concept of *virtus* he did not admit the notion of *nobilitas*, as witness C. Calpurnius Piso: 'He, a descendant of the Calpurnian family and through his father's nobility uniting in himself many famous families, was celebrated in popular gossip for *virtus* or, at least, for showy appearances which resembled *virtutes*. For he exercised his eloquence in protecting his fellow citizens, his liberality in the service of his friends and he spoke and dealt courteously even with strangers. In addition he possessed the gifts of fortune: he was tall and his face handsome. But seriousness of character and temperance in pleasure were completely lacking; he gave himself up to frivolity and ostentation and at times to debauchery, which was approved by the majority who, in view of the great sweetness of vice, do not wish the highest power to be strict or austere.'[26] Similarly the emperor Galba, who came of an ancient noble family, Tacitus judged as having lacked vices rather than possessed *virtutes*. His high birth and the terror of the times led men to call in him wisdom what was really indolence.[27] *Virtus* and *nobilitas* were disjoined, as among the Germans who chose their kings for nobility and their generals for *virtus*.[28] They had nothing to do with each other; the nobles must prove by their own personal *virtus*, which was all that mattered, whether they were worthy of their ancestors.[29]

In adopting this position Tacitus was following a line of thought that can be traced back as far as Cato the Censor in the second century BC. Yet it was not without relevance to the political developments in the century or so that separated him from Virgil, Horace and Livy.

By the time of Tacitus the Republican nobility was all but extinct and those few families which remained were remote from political power. The principal agents of the decline of the *nobiles* were the civil wars which ended in the dictatorship of Caesar and which broke out again after his death and the homicidal proclivities of the Julio-Claudian dynasty.[30] No battle was so murderous to the nobility as that at Philippi. Brutus and Cassius fell and with them the son of Cato, the younger Hortensius, a Lucullus, a Livius Drusus and Sex. Quinctilius Varus.[31] After Philippi the names of the Hortensii, the Luculli, the Lutatii, the Servilii Caepiones, the Calpurnii Bibuli and, perhaps, the Porcii Catones are found no more in the lists of consuls.[32] Members of the aristocracy joined Octavian only when it appeared that he might prove more powerful than Antony. After Actium, as Tacitus put it, those *nobiles* who had escaped death in battle or the proscriptions 'were exalted by wealth and office, as each was ready for slavery, and as they had grown great on revolution they preferred the present dispensation and safety to the old order and danger'.[33] Yet the *nobiles* were the natural enemies of the Princeps. Under Augustus perished the last of the Cornelii Scipiones and the last of the Claudii Pulchri, accused of adultery with the Princeps' daughter, Julia. The same charge carried off Iullus Antonius, the son of Mark Antony, and secured the banishment of Ti. Sempronius Gracchus, later killed in exile. Two Aemilii, the son of the triumvir Lepidus and L. Aemilius Paullus, were executed for conspiracy. Nor did Augustus spare his own family. His daughter, granddaughter and grandson all were banished. Having removed its nearest rivals the imperial dynasty, uniting eventually the blood of Julii, Claudii, Antonii and Domitii Ahenobarbi, turned under the later emperors to rend itself. To Nero succeeded the Patrician Ser. Sulpicius Galba, a disaster.[34] The next emperor was a new man, the son of a tax collector.[35] By the time of Trajan and Hadrian descendants of Republican *nobiles* were portentously rare in political life. Hadrian executed C. Calpurnius Piso Frugi Licinianus. A member of another branch of the same family was consul in AD 111. The Acilii Glabriones fantastically survived even into the next century with consuls in the direct line in AD 210 and 256. But when Juvenal mocked the value of pedigrees, his examples, the descendants of the Republican nobility, were dead and of no account.[36] The decline and fall of the *nobiles* was, clearly, a theme which fascinated Tacitus. In the *Annales*, writing of a period when there still was a nobility, he recorded the process in detail.[37] It was not a mean or unimportant subject, the demise of a great and glorious aristocracy which had built Rome and her empire—and destroyed the Republic.

The Republican nobility, operating a policy of carefully controlled inclusion of new men, long held the majority of the peoples of Italy from citizenship and office at Rome. Civil strife swiftly supervening on the Social war first retarded and then accelerated the rise of men from the newly enfranchised parts of Italy. Their first consulates came with civil war and Caesar: P. Vatinius of the Marsi, suffect consul in 47 BC, A. Hirtius and P. Ventidius, consuls in 43, C. Asinius Pollio, consul in 40. Caesar, it was said, admitted into the Senate centurions and soldiers, scribes and the sons of freedmen and, the ultimate disgrace, Gauls who knew neither the Latin language nor the whereabouts of the Senate-house and who were more at home in barbarian trousers than the Roman tunic.[38] The allegations were libellous, in a traditional way. Only one centurion can be detected among Caesar's new senators and the Gauls, it may be assumed, came from the anomalous and Romanized province of Gallia Cisalpina, the home of Catullus, Virgil and Livy. The majority of the new senators came from the local aristocracies of the municipalities of Italy, men of a class largely represented in the Senate ever since the time of Sulla. The policy of Caesar was an intensification of that of the nobility at large, but it brought a social and political revolution. Octavian relied almost exclusively at first on new men from the municipalities, men like Maecenas, Agrippa, Salvidienus Rufus, Statilius Taurus. Salvidienus fell victim to his own ambition and indiscretion, but the rest went on with Octavian to wealth and power. The system of Augustus rested on a coalition of nobles and new men with the new men, especially those who had risen under the restored Republic, predominating in positions of power. The transformation of the political oligarchy was not to be contained by geography. Long before Actium Cornelius Balbus became consul, in 40 BC. A portentous figure, he came not from any town of Italy, not even from the civilized part of Gaul south of the river Po, not even from a respectable colony or settlement of Italians, but from Cadiz in Spain. Another Cornelius, Gallus, fought in the revolutionary wars, composed poetry and was the first governor of Egypt for Augustus. His origin was from Fréjus in Narbonese Gaul. He was the descendant not of a Roman or Italian migrant but of a native dynastic family. Under Caligula two men from Narbonese Gaul reached the consulship, Valerius Asiaticus in 35, Domitius Afer in 39. Both were of native Gallic stock and Valerius achieved the ultimate distinction of a second consulate in 46 under Claudius. Caligula was interested in Gaul and the promotion of its inhabitants.[39] So too was Claudius. As censor in AD 48 he decided to add a number of Gallic nobles to the Senate. Tacitus reports the scene and chance has preserved the greater part of Claudius' speech on a bronze tablet found at Lyons.[40] According to Tacitus the emperor's proposal provoked a deputation of Roman nobles. Italy, they said, was not so sick that it could not furnish a senate for its own capital city. Once Roman senators had satisfied the peoples of Italy with whom they were related by blood. Even today the examples which the Roman character had achieved by its old ways were quoted as incitements to *virtus* and *gloria*. Why should the traditional and recent enemies of Rome capture the Senate-house and deprive the noble and the small senator from Latium of their rightful honours? Let the Gauls be citizens, if they must, but the insignia of the senators and the glories of the magistracies were too precious to be shared promiscuously. The emperor was unconvinced. Tacitus' Claudius replies with a remorseless and erudite dissertation on the history of the ruling class at Rome from Romulus and the Etruscan kings through the immigration of new families during the Republic to Cornelius Balbus. He concludes with an appeal to the elasticity and dynamism of the Roman tradition: 'Everything, senators, which is now believed ancient was once new: after Patrician magistrates came plebeian; after plebeian, Latin; after Latin, magistrates from the other nations of Italy. This present proposal too will become old and what today we defend by precedents will itself be counted among precedents.' Tacitus has condensed and dignified the actual words of Claudius as we have them from the Lyon Bronze, made them worthy of the theme which was more important even than that of the decline of the nobility. The future was on Claudius' side. But there is no evidence that he accelerated the revolution. Yet the process went inexorably on. Seneca from Corduba in Spain and Burrus from Gallic Vasio watched over the young Nero, attempted to divert his worst excesses into channels less harmful to the state and ruled the world for him. Augustus had governed with an uneasy and mutually suspicious alliance of nobles and new men. Vespasian, himself a new man from Italy, was supported by a ruling oligarchy composed of municipal Italians and aristocrats from the provinces. Under him men like M. Ulpius Traianus from Spain and Cn. Iulius Agricola from Fréjus not merely reached the Senate but were numbered among the Patricians. The first stage of the process culminated in the elevation of Trajan, a Spaniard married to a woman from Nîmes in Gaul, to the supreme power. But it did not stop there. Africa produced her first consul probably in AD 80. Ten years later the first consul from Asia is recorded.[41] Between the accession of Hadrian and the death of Commodus men from Africa and the East caught and perhaps overtook those from Italy and the West in numbers of senators if not in numbers of consuls.[42]

The new men had triumphed and with them their concept of *virtus*. The qualities they professed were those praised long ago by Cato the Censor and which had become traditional in the thought and advertisement of the *novi homines*. Of them Tacitus wrote 'the new men from the municipalities and colonies and even from the provinces who were frequently recruited into the Senate brought with them the frugality they practised at home and although by fortune or hard work they arrived at a rich old age, they nevertheless retained their former attitude.'[43] Frugality was an ancient virtue.[44] It had vanished from the capital but it remained in the distant country towns and in those parts of Italy which austerely still retained the ancient ways and from which came men unused to debauchery or degrading adulation.[45] It remained, too, in the provinces.[46] Just so had Cato talked almost three centuries before.

But for all their parade of merit and antique virtue, a difficulty remained. No less than the *nobiles* the *novi homines*, traditionally, competed for *gloria*. Yet to all such competition the imperial system was inimical. The hostility of the times to the *virtutes* on which *gloria* was based is a recurrent theme in Tacitus' works.[47] Mediocrity was at a premium. Tiberius in his choice of provincial governors did not seek outstanding *virtutes*, but, on the other hand, he hated vice: from the best he feared danger to himself, from the worst public scandal.[48] In the post-Neronian chaos nobility, wealth, offices refused or held gave ground for accusations and to display *virtutes* brought most certain death.[49] As for Domitian, like Caligula he was a bitter foe of *virtutes* and *gloria*.[50] His greatest fear was that the fame of a subject should exceed that of the emperor. His suppression of forensic eloquence and the distinguished accomplishments of civil life would have been in vain if anyone but himself laid hold of military *gloria*. Other achievements might more easily somehow or other be depreciated: the *virtus* of a good general belonged to the emperor.[51] A Tiberius or a Nero, a Caligula or a Domitian might aggravate the problem but, in truth, it was inherent in the nature of the imperial system under good emperors as under bad. *Gloria* and *virtus* created enemies for themselves since they indicted their opposites too closely and to all rulers *virtus* and boldness in their subjects was displeasing.[52] Displeasing because dangerous and military *virtus* and *gloria*, as Tacitus noted, were most dangerous of all. Politics could be stifled, civil affairs controlled: the army made and unmade emperors.

The imperial system was a fact. Only thus could the great mass of empire stand in balance and be prevented from lapsing into chaos at the hands of a people who, if they could not endure complete slavery, could not bear complete political liberty either.[53] The lesson of Tacitus' treatment of Galba, Otho and Vitellius is that for stability a strong monarchy was essential. Since it existed the empire must be governed. Public service, now as under the Republic, was the duty of men of proper status and attainments. Retreat from reality, however harsh, was shameful. Tacitus attacked those who cloaked a useless idleness under the high-sounding name of philosophic contemplation of higher things.[54] Equally he attacked irresponsibility, the ostentatious deaths which did the state no good or the ruinous display of a useless liberty.[55] As always in the Roman tradition, the *respublica* must be served.

It was, as we have already seen, a convention to criticize Roman faults or prescribe their remedies by exhibiting the virtues of remote places and foreign tribes. Tacitus' *Germania* conformed to the convention. It was not merely that the virtues and habits of the Germans corresponded to the traditional *mores* of Rome.[56] There was a political lesson too. 'When they join battle it is shameful for the chief (*princeps*) to be surpassed in *virtus* and shameful for his retinue not to equal the *virtus* of the chief. Indeed, the man who leaves the battle alive when his chief has been killed suffers lifelong infamy and opprobrium. The essence of their oath is to defend him, protect him and to attribute to his *gloria* their own brave deeds. The chiefs fight for victory, their companions for their chief.'[57]

Gloria was to be no longer the pursuit of individual preeminence ruinous to individual and state alike.[58] It was to be tempered by obedience, *obsequium*, above all a military virtue. Public men must act as soldiers, winning by their deeds in the service of the state such glory as was consistent with their position, but obedient always to their commander, the emperor.[59] The most detailed portrait of the type is to be found in Tacitus' biography of his father-in-law, Cn. Iulius Agricola. Agricola was born in AD 40 in the ancient colony at Fréjus in Gaul of a family with a tradition of public service.[60] His father, a senator, possibly reached the praetorship but soon after Agricola's birth he fell foul of Caligula and was executed. Agricola, therefore, was brought up by his mother who put him through a rigorous course of intellectual and moral education. He attended the university at Marseilles, a place which nicely combined Greek civilization and the rough frugality traditionally typical of the provinces. 'I remember', wrote Tacitus, 'that he often said that in his youth he was more deeply attracted to philosophy than was proper for a Roman and a senator.'[61] We notice the abiding Roman prejudice against the study of philosophy as an end in itself. The same note appears in Tacitus' historical works with regard to men like Helvidius and Thrasea.[62] It is the same position as we find in Cicero. Philosophy may confirm a man's resolution and broaden his outlook, but it is praiseworthy only in so far as it assists a man to perform his proper function, participation in public life and the government of the *respublica*. Agricola, however, was saved by his mother. After this false start in the pursuit of *gloria*, he applied himself to a public career.[63] He saw his first military service in Britain under Suetonius Paulinus and already exhibited those traits which were to mark his later career. He did not take his tour of duty, as so many young officers did, as a holiday, but, showing himself neither licentious nor lazy, he applied himself assiduously to the military art. Although the direction of the war was in the hands of another and the *gloria* went to his general, Agricola's experiences nevertheless fired him too with a desire for *gloria*, despite the fact that in those times eminence was dangerous and a reputation for greatness as perilous as one for evil.[64] His next overseas appointment was as quaestor to the governor of Asia, Salvius Titianus. Once more Agricola took the path of virtue. He was corrupted neither by the seductive allurements of the province nor by the compliant greed of his governor. On his return to Rome he retired into private life. The last years of Nero's reign were one of the few periods when the greatest fault in a man of the senatorial class, non-involvement in public affairs, *inertia*, could be counted wisdom. Agricola performed the duties of tribune and praetor in the same spirit, steering a middle course between economy and extravagance, between reasonableness and lavishness. Entrusted by Galba with the important task of checking the temple treasures after the Neronian depredations, he acted with energy and diligence.[65] Agricola passed the year of the four emperors safely and emerged, in due season, commanding the twentieth legion for Vespasian. Once more Agricola displayed moderation in playing down his restoration of discipline among the disaffected troops.[66] The twentieth legion was stationed in Britain, then under the governorship of Vettius Bolanus, to whose pacific nature Agricola, skilled in obedience, tempered his ambitions. The replacement of Vettius by Petilius Cerialis gave more scope for his talents. But Agricola received *gloria* as a gift from his commander and, like the Germans, was always careful to ascribe his success to Petilius who had originated the plans and whose servant he was. 'Thus by *virtus* in obedience, by modesty in speech he escaped jealousy but won *gloria*.'[67] Agricola returned to Rome and his reward. Vespasian enrolled him among the Patricians and put him in charge of the peaceful province of Aquitania. Here too he displayed his natural prudence. Upright and pure, he did not seek fame by showing off his *virtus* or by artifice. After less than three years he was recalled to the consulate and the governorship of Britain.[68] The campaigns of the next seven years need not detain us. Agricola had left Rome in the last year of Vespasian's reign. He returned to the rule of Domitian. His good sense did not desert him. His real victories contrasted with the emperor's mock triumph over Germany and he knew Domitian's attitude to *gloria*, especially military *gloria*, in others. Consequently he entered Rome secretly by night and studiously cultivated retirement and non-involvement in affairs. Thus he survived, but without further distinction or employment. In the wars in Dacia, Moesia, Germany and Pannonia he was not found a command. Further, it was represented to him that he should forego his claim to the proconsulate of Asia or Africa. Agricola complied with a moderation and prudence which softened even the implacable irascibility of Domitian. 'Neither by perverse obstinacy nor by an empty display of liberty did he challenge renown and ruin.'[69]

The *Life of Agricola* is a complex work. A laudatory biography, it at the same time forms an apologia for men like Tacitus who had not merely survived but had co-operated with and received advancement from the tyranny of Domitian.[70] Not itself a revolutionary document, it nevertheless is a document of a revolution. The *Agricola* expounds the moral and political ideas of the new aristocracy, not systematically formulated but emerging gradually in the portrayal of an individual and in the stages of a senator's career.[71]

Gloria with moderation and prudence, obedience and subordination: the Republican noble would have termed it slavery. Tacitus was aware of it and turned on the *nobiles* their own propaganda. If they were enslaved it was their own doing. After the fiercest spirits had fallen in battle or in the proscriptions, the rest of the nobility had cheerfully accepted slavery in return for wealth and office.[72] Tacitus has left on record Tiberius' disgust. That emperor, nothing if not an aristocrat, was accustomed to remark as he left the senate-house 'How ready these men are for slavery!' Not that he desired the return of Republican liberty in public affairs.[73] Neither a ferocious display of independence, dangerous to the *respublica* no less than to the individual, nor the corrupting excesses of servile adulation were needed. A middle course combining reasonable glory with rational obedience was entirely possible—and demanded by the needs of the state. Tacitus exemplified it in the careers of men like Agricola and Seneca and in minor characters too, like M. Lepidus under Tiberius. Of him Tacitus wrote, 'I discover that this Lepidus was for that period a serious and wise man; for to many senatorial motions he gave a better turn, away from the brutal adulation of others. He did not, however, lack discretion, since he was powerfully and uniformly in influence and favour with Tiberius. Consequently I am compelled to doubt whether the favour of emperors to some and their hostility to others is ruled by fate and our lot at birth, like everything else, or whether some power resides in our own decisions and it is possible to walk a road free of ambition and danger between harsh obstinacy and vile obsequiousness'.[74] Then there was Memmius Regulus whose authority, firmness and reputation brought him the greatest possible glory under the shadow of the emperor's high position. He was a resource for the *respublica*; even Nero admitted it.[75] It is revealing of Tacitus' methods and attitudes that he put a direct and forceful statement of the position into the mouth of a villain, Eprius Marcellus. Marcellus remembered the form of government established by their fathers and grandfathers; he also remembered the times in which he was born. He admired the past and followed the present. He prayed for good emperors, but put up with any sort. It was all very well for Helvidius to be compared with men like Cato and Brutus in firmness and courage: for himself, he was only one of the Senate and they were all slaves. The worst emperors wanted unlimited domination; even the best desired a limit to the freedom of their subjects.[76] Pliny went further than Tacitus. *Obsequium* conferred *gloria* and was the key which opened the door to the highest power. It was by his *obsequium* under Domitian that Trajan achieved the Principate.[77]

A superficial pessimism formed the principal intellectual equipment of most Roman historians. Change and decay were everywhere and the two terms were considered synonymous. Things were never what they had once been. It is not the least of Tacitus' merits that he refused assent to the easy and fraudulent simplification: 'Luxury of the table which was practised at prodigal expense throughout the hundred years between the end of the war of Actium and the battles in which Ser. Galba secured power gradually went out of fashion. The causes of this change may be investigated. Once noble families of wealth and outstanding fame were undermined by their passion for splendour. For even then it was still permitted to court and be courted by the people, Rome's allies and the client kings. The more showy a man was in his wealth, house and way of life, the more glorious he was considered through his fame and clientele. After the brutality of the executions, when greatness of reputation meant death, those who remained turned to wiser courses. At the same time new men from the municipalities and colonies and even from the provinces who were frequently recruited into the Senate brought to Rome the frugality they had practised at home and although by fortune or hard work many of them arrived at a rich old age, nevertheless their earlier cast of mind remained. But Vespasian was the outstanding originator of the strict moral code, himself a man of antique way of life. Therefore obedience to the emperor and love of emulating him were stronger than the penalties of the law and fear. Unless, perhaps, there resides in all things a kind of cycle so that as the changes of the seasons revolve, so too there are similar revolutions in morals. Nor was everything better among our ancestors, but our age too has produced many examples of fame and ability worthy to be imitated by posterity. May we retain this honourable competition with our ancestors.'[78]

CHAPTER V

THE DEFENCE OF ROMANIA

'At the moment when Rome, who will endure as long as men live, with her first auspices rose into the light of the world, that she might grow with the greatest increase, virtus *and Fortune, frequently at variance, agreed in a treaty of eternal peace. If either had failed, she would not have come as she has to perfect supremacy.'*[1]

THE ESTABLISHMENT of the Principate abolished politics. But not all at once or at one stroke. Rather, open politics declined as the passage of years and events revealed the true nature of the new order. The ferocious independence of the Republican nobility was restrained, as it had to be, at the start, by Augustus. Yet, for the rest, even under Nero it was possible for Seneca to take charge of events and to attempt to ameliorate the excesses of the emperor or to divert them into channels less harmful to the state. With the abolition of the Republican notion of political liberty went a change in the arena of political activity. It was no longer in the Senate-house and assemblies of the Roman People that the important decisions were reached or, at least, advertised, but in the council and entourage of the emperor. Under such conditions, the apparatus of the *respublica*, the Senate and the magistrates, became largely decorative and the distinction between politics and intrigue, always faint, irretrievably blurred. Tacitus bears witness to the first stage of the process: all power resided with the emperor who could share it with others or keep it to himself as he wished. The best a public man could do was to avoid the intrigues of the court and to offer himself as a loyal and upright servant of the state. The politician gave place to the administrator.

It had been the fashion at least from the time of Cicero to describe Rome as a bilge, sink or cesspool into which flowed all that was most depraved and corrupt from Italy and the provinces.[2] Greek and Asiatic men and manners were held up to particular contempt. Tacitus displayed all the prejudice of the imperial race against Greeks and Jews. 'I cannot bear a Greek Rome', screamed Juvenal.[3] Yet it was the wealth and revenues of the East that had nourished and supported Rome and the West. The division of the Roman empire, adumbrated in the dispositions of Octavian and Antony, corresponded to a real distinction in prosperity, language and culture. In Spain and Gaul it was Rome herself who by conquest brought civilization to barbaric tribes and undeveloped lands. In Greece, Asia and Egypt she met high culture already established and material resources that far outstripped her own. What is remarkable is not that the Roman empire eventually split into two parts, but that it held together so long as it did. Octavian and Antony had already shown the way, yet it was not until sixty-five years after the foundation of Constantinople that the break between East and West was finally consummated. The end of the Republic had brought a widening in the governing class at Rome, explosive in the Triumviral Period, more gradual but relentless under the early Empire. More and more provincials were drawn into the government. With the accession of Trajan the provincials captured the imperial position itself. Trajan was a provincial, it is true, from the Spanish province of Baetica. But he was no upstart. His home town was Italica, founded by Scipio Africanus to settle his veterans during the war with Hannibal. Trajan's father had commanded a legion under Vespasian in the Jewish war, governed Syria and received the proconsulate of Asia, the pinnacle of a senatorial career, and the ornaments of a triumph.[4] Trajan, it is clear, was not essentially different from the Republican *novi homines* from Italy, such as Cn. Octavius, consul in 165 BC. But the pressure from the highly developed and cultured East was great. Towards the end of the first century AD Greeks and Asiatics begin to appear in the lists of consuls. Their presence is indicative of a greater number in the lower reaches of the Senate and the imperial administration. But the Senate remained not merely western but predominantly Italian. At the accession of Trajan perhaps as much as three-quarters of the membership of the Senate was of Italian origin. Although by the death of Marcus Aurelius in AD 180 Italian representation had declined to something like half the total, the Greek East was still grossly underrepresented. To the end of the Roman empire in the west men of western origin predominated in power, if not in actual numbers, in the Senate at Rome.

The Senate had long since ceased to be an effective organ of government. Already under Augustus and his immediate successors the senators, from motives not all dishonourable, had resigned the real conduct of affairs to the emperor. The passage of time intensified this tendency. Ammianus Marcellinus records few actions of the Senate as a body, only one that was contrary to the emperor's wishes.[5] The account of the 'debate' in the Roman Senate on the promulgation of the Theodosian Code reads like nothing so much as a report of the proceedings of one of the more decorative but impressively named governmental bodies in modern Russia or China. The senators occupied them selves with shouting slogans such as 'Through you we hold our honours, our property, everything!', repeated twenty-eight times, and 'To prevent the constitutions being interpolated let all the codes be written in long-hand!', repeated twenty-five times.[6] Yet membership of the senatorial order still bestowed the highest dignity, which very fact may have contributed not a little to the loss even of those vestiges of political power which the Senate still retained. To confer honour and dignity men were granted senatorial rank, with the consequence that the size of the Senate was greatly enlarged. Under Diocletian the Senate at Rome numbered, probably, about six hundred members. When Constantine founded the complementary Senate of Constantinople, it was a small and select body. By AD 357 it had three hundred members; thirty years later its size had risen to no fewer than two thousand members. This explosive expansion reflected a similar, but more gradual, process at Rome. It was achieved, in the main, by increasing the number of offices which automatically granted senatorial rank, by shortening the normal tenure of these offices, by granting membership of the Senate to an increasing number of palace officials and by honorary awards. Clearly few of these senators would be in constant attendance at the meetings of the Roman Senate. Many were not even domiciled in Italy. Trajan had already been aware of the problem posed by the geographical expansion of the senatorial order when he enacted that senators should invest one-third of their capital in Italian land in the belief that it was improper that those who sought office at Rome should look on Italy not as their native land but as a lodging on their journeys.[7] It remained a technical obligation for the senators in the late Empire to reside in Rome or Constantinople. But, although many of the older families retained some physical connection with Rome, by the early fourth century most senators resided permanently in the provinces.

The decline in the importance of the Roman Senate, except for decoration and honour, mirrored a decline in the importance of Rome herself. Since all power resided with the emperor, the capital was where he happened to be. The nobility of the late Republic had been Rome-centred to the point of criminal neglect of the needs of the empire. The Julio-Claudians, as befitted their ancestry, were essentially men of Rome. Their absences from the capital, demanded by military necessity, administrative needs or the powerful stimulus of vainglory, were, on the whole, brief. But the year AD 69 showed the truth that emperors could be made elsewhere than at Rome. That year exhibited a decisive shift in power and consummated a process that had begun in the late second century BC. Marius had created the conditions for the development of the client army, which was used first to influence voting in the Assemblies and then for direct military intervention in politics. The rise of the military dynasts in the first century BC carried with it a rise in the power of the armies themselves. Like civil politicians, the military men were powerless without their clients. In the year of the four emperors the military clients realized their power to create their own patrons. Yet the army was less a disruptive force than has sometimes been imagined. Its loyalty lay with its patron, the emperor, and his family. The history of the first four centuries of the Roman imperial system, despite the military anarchy of the third century AD, clearly demonstrates the adherence of the army to the hereditary principle. Ammianus shows the usurper Procopius securing the loyalty of the troops in Thrace by taking in his arms the daughter of Constantius, exhibiting her to the soldiers and claiming kinship with the dead emperor.[8] The same plea won over the army sent against him by Valens. The revolt was suppressed only by the authority of Arbitio, one of Constantine's generals, and the appearance of Valens himself.

The military anarchy of the third century, the loss of the Eastern provinces and the disintegration of Roman Europe not merely demonstrated the power and importance of the army; it also caused far-reaching and permanent social and economic changes. The peculiar nature of society and government in the fourth century was the result of the attempts of successive emperors, notably Diocletian and Constantine, building on the recovery of the empire by Gallienus, Claudius, Aurelian and Probus, and intensifying trends long apparent, to hold together the empire under a central authority. In place of the old distinction between senatorial and equestrian careers combining both civil and military functions, which went back to Augustus, the civil administration was divided sharply from the military. Both were under the direct control of the emperor, who ruled largely by edict. The civil administration consisted chiefly in a palace bureaucracy, which, like all bureaucracies, proliferated. The Senate and the magistracies, though they continued to exist, were replaced by the government of a totalitarian despot ruling through a cumbersome and inefficient bureaucracy and buttressed by one of the most repressive codes of law ever created. To ensure internal stability society was regimented by an elaborate class system. Yet, under Diocletian and his successors the government of the Roman empire remained what it had always been, essentially aristocratic and oligarchic. The chief posts in the government tended to be filled by members of an aristocracy which, though different in composition from that of the Republic and Principate, yet stood in direct spiritual succession to the old *nobiles*. Indeed, some of the greater houses claimed direct physical descent from the nobility of the Republic. Scepticism is a natural and inevitable reaction, but the claims were accepted by contemporaries and it is not beyond all possibility that they could be established by the tortuous bypaths of adoption and descent in the female line. This aristocracy, prominent in the Senate, the emperor's consistory and the offices of the administration, disposed of considerable power and could even check the greater power of the emperor.

For the fourth century AD we are fortunate in possessing the evidence of Ammianus Marcellinus.[9] It is true that the extant portion of his *History* covers barely twenty-five years from the winter of 353–354 to the battle of Adrianople in 378. But Ammianus would be counted a good historian in any company; among Roman historians he stands out as a great one. From his judgement of men and events a coherent set of principles emerges, centering on the notion of the *respublica.* The old term continued in use, as pliable and evocative as ever. Not that Ammianus envisaged any alternative to the imperial system; there is no hint of that nor is it to be expected. The system had endured through many modifications and adaptations for four centuries. It was a fact of life and Ammianus accepted it as such. For him revolution meant merely the forcible replacement of an emperor by a usurper. It was not merely that the Principate hardening into despotism had abolished the trafficking in governmental systems. The chief issue of Ammianus' time was more imperative than the disputation of the niceties of the distribution of power. The struggle was now not for power at Rome or the emperor's court, but for the survival of Rome herself and the civilization and culture for which she stood, for all, that is, that was comprehended in the idea and ideal of *Romania.* This notion made its first appearance in the first half of the fourth century and completed a process which originated far back in the Republic. The expansion of Roman power in Italy and the pressure of foreign invaders such as the Gauls and Pyrrhus gave rise to the first sentiments of Italian unity. These sentiments grew slowly and even more slowly and hesitantly grew the concept that Italy and Rome formed a unity. The process did not stop with the realization of this unity under Augustus. The Roman provinces were brought in, just as they were brought in to the expansion of the ruling class. The edict of Caracalla, though its practical effect may have been small, recognized the essential unity of the whole Roman world and its separation from the nations which surrounded it. It was for this idea that *Romania* stood. It defined all the inhabitants of the Roman empire, the *Romani*, as a distinct nation, which despite all internal ethnic and cultural differences, possessed an essential unity and a common way of life which divided it sharply from the barbarians.[10] The defence of *Romania* both as an ideal and in the sense of the preservation of the territorial integrity of the empire is the true subject of Ammianus' *History*. The struggle to preserve *Romania* from the outside forces that would destroy it took place not beyond the boundaries of a stable and peaceful empire, but more and more within the provinces themselves. To the impending collapse of Roman control in the provinces Ammianus bears abundant testimony. We learn that Pamphylia, though far removed from the frontiers of the empire, was protected under Constantius by a network of forts and garrisons against plundering raids and massacres.[11] The whole of southern Asia Minor, in fact, seems to have suffered regularly from the depredations of Isaurian bandits who pillaged the rich country estates and even attacked the towns, including Seleucia.[12] Similar brigandage is recorded in Syria in AD 369.[13] Under such conditions it is not surprising that the food supply was uncertain, even for Antioch, one of the major cities of the empire.[14] In the west the situation was the same. That Britain should have suffered incursions by the Picts and Scots is not remarkable.[15] But Gaul, according to Ammianus, had endured long neglect and by AD 355 was the scene of massacre, plunder and arson, with the barbarians pillaging as they wished. This state of affairs continued until, at least, AD 369, under which year Ammianus records the death in a bandit ambush of Constantianus, brother of the wife of the emperor Valentinian.[16] In 357 the Danubian provinces of Raetia, Valeria, Moesia and Pannonia were raided by the Suebi, Quadi and Sarmatae.[17] Africa, likewise, from the beginning of the reign of Valentinian was plundered by the barbarians and the Roman army did little to prevent it.[18]

These conditions, the inability of the Roman army to control the countryside and continuous brigandage from within the provinces and from without, were a standing invitation to invasion by more powerful enemies, such as the king of Persia. Immediately after the elevation by Valentinian of Valens as his colleague in the imperial power, Ammianus wrote, 'as though the trumpets were sounding for war throughout the whole Roman world, the most savage tribes rose and leaped across the frontiers of empire nearest to them. The Alamanni plundered the provinces of Gaul and Raetia; the Sarmatae and Quadi those of Pannonia; the Picts, Saxons and Scots with the Atacotti devastated Britain with continuous disasters; the Austoriani and other Moorish tribes invaded Africa more fiercely than usual' (a phrase to be noted!); 'plundering bands of Goths devastated Thrace. The king of Persia threw bands of troops into Armenia, hastening with excessive violence to bring it into his power once again.'[19] The whole year, Ammianus judged, afflicted the Roman state with grievous losses.

With the fate of Rome and with the ideal of *Romania* Ammianus was passionately involved. Throughout he insisted on the continuity of Roman history, that the state which was now fighting desperately for existence was the same as that which had defeated Hannibal and first conquered the Mediterranean world. He saw a clear line of succession from the early kings to the great heroes of the Republic; from them to Pompey and Caesar, to Cicero and the younger Cato; from them, again, to Domitius Corbulo and Trajan and thence through the great soldier-emperors of the third century, Claudius and Aurelian, to his own time. To Ammianus Rome's past was always present and relevant to his subject. This appears, above all, in his incessant habit of annotating the events he recorded by examples and parallels from earlier Roman history. That the disaster at Adrianople should be compared to that at Cannae is, perhaps, not remarkable; Cannae had long ago become the archetypal Roman defeat, sanctified by literary tradition. But the sheer number of Ammianus' Roman examples not merely displays the author's erudition, not only testifies to the typically Greek thoroughness of his research methods, but proclaims his belief that what was being defended in the later fourth century was not some latter-day upstart state but in very truth the *respublica* of Cincinnatus and the Decii, of the two Africani and both the Catones, of Cicero and Caesar, of Corbulo and Lusius Quietus.[20]

To Ammianus the contemporary inhabitants of the city of Rome appeared indolent, frivolous and corrupt. Early in his *History* as we have it he made his apology: 'I think that some foreigners' (it is noteworthy that Ammianus, though a Greek from the East, here wrote as though he were a Roman of Rome) 'who perhaps will read this history, if it should so happen, will wonder why, when my discourse turns to describe affairs at Rome, nothing is narrated except riots, taverns and other similar frivolities.'[21] He did not exaggerate. All he has to record of events at Rome are disorder, the names of officials, the prevalence of vice and the corruption of justice.[22] Yet for the ideal of Rome Ammianus had the utmost reverence. His animadversion on the nature of Roman affairs leads to a résumé of the history of the city: 'Her people from the beginnings of their infancy to the end of their childhood, which was about three hundred years, endured wars around its walls; then, when it had grown up, after many varied troubles in war they crossed the Alps and the sea; having attained the strength of manhood, they won laurels and triumphs from every shore which the great earth surrounds; now, when they are declining into old age and often conquer by their name alone, it has retired to a quieter way of life. So the venerable city after the arrogant necks of uncivilized tribes had been humbled, after laws, the eternal foundations and moorings of liberty, had been passed, like a frugal, wise and rich parent entrusted the administration of the rights of her inheritance to the Caesars as to her children. And, although the tribes have long been in retirement and the centuries at peace and there are no electoral contests, but the stability of the time of Pompilius has returned, in all the regions of the world she is taken as mistress and queen and everywhere the white hair and prestige of the senators are reverenced and the name of the Roman people regarded with respect and awe.'[23] To explain Rome's greatness Ammianus put himself squarely in a tradition that went back to the Republic in the invocation of *virtus* and Fortune which stands at the head of this chapter.[24] Towards Fortune the Romans had always had a double attitude. On the one hand, Fortune was seen as blind and capricious chance against whose machinations no man could provide and who could rob even the man of *virtus* of the just rewards of his merits. Since she was utterly irrational, Fortune's gifts, however desirable, were evanescent and deluding. On the other hand, however, the favour of Fortune implied the favour of the gods and the man or state in which Fortune and *virtus* were joined was the most blessed and successful. Thus Livy put into the mouth of Romulus the saying 'Cities, like everything else, are born in the lowest estate; then those whom their own *virtus* and the gods assist create wealth and great fame for themselves: know that at the birth of Rome the gods were present and the *virtus* of her citizens will not fail.'[25] Almost at the end of the Roman empire in the west, Ammianus, writing barely a decade before the sack of Rome by Alaric, yet asserted the same tradition: Rome was founded by the favour of the gods who have made her great and by whose eternal help she will stand forever unshaken.[26] With the idea of *virtus* Ammianus was not obsessed as Sallust had been nor was he even concerned, like Tacitus, consciously to reinterpret the ideal to suit new conditions. But from his *History* a concept of *virtus* emerges which is clearly in direct line of descent from the aristocratic ideal of the Republic. For instance, Ammianus' judgement on Hypatius as 'from the beginning of his youth commended by the beauty of his *virtutes*, a man of quiet and peaceful counsel, exactly weighing the honourableness of his gentle ways, who brought *gloria* to the fame of his ancestors and himself honoured his posterity by the admirable acts of his two prefectures' recalls in language and sentiment the Republican epitaphs.[27] Again, Constantius was tormented by the *virtutes* of Julian 'which ever increasing report was pouring forth through the mouths of various nations, carrying the exalted glories of his great labours and deeds after certain kingdoms of Alamannia had been subdued and Gallic towns had been recovered which had been plundered and destroyed by the barbarians whom he himself made subject to tribute and taxation'.[28] *Virtus* was a specifically Roman attribute. The city of Rome herself was the tutelar deity of empire and of all the *virtutes*.[29] It was the ancient, sober Roman *virtus* which had enabled the men of old to overcome all difficulties posed by men and nature.[30] Nowhere in his *History* does Ammianus directly attribute *virtus* to non-Romans. When it is used of Rome's enemies, on both occasions it occurs in reports of their words and Ammianus deliberately draws attention to their arrogance. The Alamanni 'sent envoys and imperiously enough ordered the Caesar to get out of the lands they had won for themselves by *virtus* and the sword'. Sapor, king of Persia, in the course of an imperious correspondence with Constantius, made a traditional Roman boast: 'That which you exultantly assert will never come to acceptance among us, that successes in war should be praised without distinction between *virtus* and trickery.'[31] Both the Alamanni and Sapor arrogated to themselves attitudes which were properly peculiar to the Romans. Both, in fact, usurped the imperial prerogative and issued orders to the Roman emperor or to his immediate deputy.

All power rested with the emperor, but he was not—or ought not to be—an arbitrary tyrant. Ammianus had a clear and definite conception of the 'legitimate emperor'. His power derived ultimately from the Roman People 'which entrusted the administration of the rights of its inheritance to the Caesars as though to its children'.[32] This notion was, in fact, constitutionally correct, though of only legalistic interest. In theory the office of emperor never became hereditary but always remained elective. It so happens that on two occasions in the period covered by Ammianus' *History*, on the deaths of Julian and Jovian, the empire was left without an emperor, a designated heir or even a surviving member of the imperial dynasty. Julian died in battle deep in enemy territory and left his army surrounded by the Persians. The day after his rather summary funeral the generals of the army and the commanders of the legions and of the cavalry held discussions on the choice of a new emperor. The discussions were inconclusive and turbulent, although in the end the aged and unwilling Salutius emerged as a compromise candidate. Then one of the soldiers of higher rank, whom Gibbon suggested to have been Ammianus himself, and he was certainly with the army, attempted to call the meeting to sense by urging that they first extricate themselves and the army and then 'if we are allowed to see Mesopotamia, the united votes of both armies' (*i.e.* of the east and west) 'will declare a legitimate emperor'. As it turned out, this diversion allowed certain hot-heads hurriedly to choose Jovian, dress him in the imperial robes and present him to the army.[33] Jovian reigned for only eight months and his death left another lacuna in the imperial succession. This time the military situation allowed more careful deliberation and 'the leaders of the civil powers and the army' at Nicaea looked for a ruler who was well proved and serious. The result of their deliberations was the choice of Valentinian after a period of ten days in which 'no one held the helm of the empire'. This choice Ammianus described as 'the decision of the whole army', but only after the leading men had decided was Valentinian produced to the army and 'after the appearance of an election was pronounced by the favourable assent of those present to be the ruler of the empire as a serious man'. Then he was proclaimed Augustus.[34] Valentinian put the imperial power into commission between himself, his brother Valens and his young son Gratian, who was only eight years old on his proclamation as Augustus in 367. Valentinian died of an apoplectic fit while on expedition in 375. Valens was far away in the East and Gratian was at Trier. To prevent trouble with the army it was decided to proclaim a new Augustus in Valentinian's place. His infant son Valentinian was 'by the unanimous decision of all' brought to the camp at Bregetio where he was 'lawfully declared emperor and announced as Augustus in due manner'.[35] Ammianus' narrative of these events makes clear his notion of the necessities for the lawful choice of a legitimate emperor: due deliberation by the leading men whose choice was then confirmed by the army. We hear nothing of confirmation of the appointments by the Senate and in the case of Valentinian II Ammianus expressly tells us that even the consent of the western emperor, Gratian, was not sought until after the election and proclamation. The elections of Jovian and Valentinian I were, however, the only two occasions on which genuine election decided the possessor of imperial power in the century and a half between the accession of Constantine and the death of Theodosius II and Valentinian III. By far the most usual method of transference of power was by *de facto*, if not *de iure*, inheritance. Before Valentinian I emperors appointed subordinate Caesars who succeeded them after due proclamation. Later emperors followed Valentinian's practice of nominating their successors as Augusti and equals during their own lifetime. Ammianus describes Valentinian as taking counsel before proclaiming Valens and thus securing a 'lawful partner in his power'.[36] Under normal conditions, the consent of the reigning emperor was the vital distinction between a legitimate ruler and a rebel. The advice of leading men and proclamation by part, at least, of the army were obtained by many usurpers. But while an Augustus remained alive, only his recognition could confer legitimacy. This Julian recognized when after his tumultuous proclamation as Augustus by his troops in Gaul he wrote to Constantius: 'Pardon me, I do not desire that these things, although they are reasonable demands, should be carried out as that you should approve them as useful and right. In the future I will eagerly support and carry out your orders.'[37] A legitimate emperor exacted by right obedience from all his subjects. Armed rebellion, being the most flagrant disobedience, was the worst of crimes. In 355 Silvanus was proclaimed Augustus at Cologne. Ammianus, who was in the staff of Ursicinus sent by Constantius to suppress the rebellion, describes in detail the machinations of Silvanus' enemies which had driven him to this desperate course. Yet Ammianus could not approve. He describes Silvanus as an upstart and Ursicinus' mission as 'to assist the necessities of the state'.[38] He shows no disapproval of the deceit by which Silvanus was first thrown off his guard and then cut down. In the case of Procopius, proclaimed emperor at Constantinople in 365, Ammianus is even more outspoken. Procopius attempted 'the most presumptuous of deeds' and his usurped position was the 'dishonour of all honours'.[39] He was a 'usurper of illegitimate power', 'traitor', 'public bandit', 'tyrant waging war on legitimate emperors'.[40] In the confusion and anger which attended his suppression, Florentius and Barchalba, who had betrayed him, were put to death. Ammianus expresses his indignation and sums up his attitude to rebellion: 'If they had betrayed a legitimate emperor, justice herself would pronounce them justly killed; if they betrayed a rebel and one who assaulted internal peace, as he was said to be, great rewards ought to have been given them for a remarkable deed.'[41]

Ammianus expected not merely that the subjects should reverence and obey the emperor, but that the emperor should have as keen a sense of the dignity and majesty of his position as he himself possessed. Ammianus consistently represents the Caesar Gallus as a vicious and savage tyrant. The emperor Constantius decided to remove him and, in order to do so without provoking civil war, sent the prefect Domitianus with instructions 'kindly and respectfully to urge Gallus to hasten to Italy'. Ammianus condemns Gallus' cruelty, yet equally he condemns Domitianus who insolently neglected to show proper deference and respect to the Caesar.[42] Further, when Gallus had finally been killed, he summed up his feelings: 'But everywhere the equity of the power of heaven was watchful. For not only did his own cruel actions overthrow Gallus but also not long afterwards the two men who had lured him into the fatal trap by softly deceiving him with treacherous tricks, although he was guilty, were carried off by excruciating deaths. Of them Scudilo had an abscess of the liver and died vomiting up his lungs; Barbatio, who had for a long time invented charges against Gallus, was charged by the whispers of certain men with aiming at higher power from his position as master of the infantry and condemned. By a lamentable death he made reparation with his life to the shades of the Caesar who had been killed through his treachery.'[43] Gallus was a monster and his execution had been ordered by the emperor. Yet even under such conditions, Ammianus held, the murder of a Caesar was an affront to divine justice. As Julian remarked on the murder of Gordian III, 'his shade did not long wander unavenged, but as though weighed in the balance of justice all those who had conspired against his life died in excruciating tortures'.[44] The emperor was the state and any harm done to him or the members of his family was a harm done to the state. In 374 the daughter of Constantius, on her way to marry Gratian, was almost captured by the Quadi. To describe the incident Ammianus employs language more appropriate, we might think, to a great military disaster. Had she been captured 'there would assuredly have happened a crime admitting of no expiation and fit to be numbered among the shameful calamities of the Roman state' and if she had been captured and ransom had been refused 'it would have branded the *respublica* with the greatest disasters'.[45] Possessing so exalted a position the emperor should behave appropriately. At the head of the necrology of Constantius Ammianus placed the observation that he always preserved the dignity of imperial prestige and authority.[46] On the other hand, it was the chief of Ammianus' complaints against Julian that he was careless of the imperial dignity. On 1 January 363 Julian went on foot with the new consuls to their inauguration. Although this was an ancient practice, Ammianus remarks that although some praised it, others criticized it as a demeaning piece of affectation. Again, Julian was a frequent attender of meetings of the Senate. On one occasion he was told that his old friend and tutor, the philosopher Maximus, had arrived from Asia and leaped from his place and ran to meet him. This action Ammianus castigates as undignified and an untimely display of affection which made Julian seem excessively desirous of empty glory.[47] In the necrology of Julian the only faults recorded are that he was talkative, superstitious rather than religious and that 'he rejoiced in the applause of the mob and had an intemperate appetite for praise even for the most trivial things. Through his desire for popularity he often stooped to talk with unworthy men.'[48] Ammianus extended this attitude even to the usurper Procopius. He dwells on the ridiculousness of the imperial robes hastily improvised for Procopius and refers as often to the laughable inadequacy of the usurper and his arrangements as to the enormity of his crime.[49] Even a usurper, Ammianus seems to suggest, ought to behave in a manner consonant with the great power he was trying impiously to attain, however criminal the attempt.

The reverence and obedience which the subjects owed to a legitimate emperor was not, for Ammianus, irrational. It was demanded for the safety of the *respublica* and was part of a mutual obligation. 'We do not deny that the safety of a legitimate emperor who is the champion and defender of good men and from whom safety is sought for others ought to be defended by the united zeal of all.'[50] The business of the emperor and the reason for his immense power was the preservation of the *Romani* and the alleviation of their troubles.[51] This being so, he should not use his absolute power as a tyrant. An emperor must avoid all excess, especially in the exercise of his power, as he would a precipice.[52] There was a distinction between lawful power and despotism.[53] Ammianus once refers to 'civil power' and once to 'civil emperors' (*civile imperium, civiles principes*).[54] By this he did not mean that the emperor should behave as a private citizen nor that his power should be exercised in civil as opposed to military affairs. Rather the imperial power was to be used in a manner befitting civilized men, rationally and in conformity with the principles of society. To act according to whim, licence and brute force was to act like a barbarian, an enemy of *Romania*. Ammianus agreed with the philosophers that power was nothing other than care for others' safety and that it was the mark of a good ruler to restrain his power, to resist desire for all things and implacable anger, to realize, as Caesar said, that the remembrance of cruelty is a miserable support for old age.[55] The emperor, in fact, must be not only legitimate but just.

Justice forms, with the military defence of *Romania*, one of the two great themes of Ammianus' *History*. The two themes are complementary and interwoven, for justice, that is, conformity to the power of law, is the mark of the civilized state as against the barbarian. Within *Romania* justice secured stability and peace. Justice and peace went hand in hand, as in the case of Cottius of Gaul who ruled his people with a just administration and, joined in alliance with the Roman state, bestowed eternal peace on his tribe.[56] But in the situation in the fourth century, Ammianus was more concerned with the absence of justice than with its presence. Julian could say 'The laws may blame my mercy but an emperor of the most lenient mind ought to rise above the other laws', but more often Ammianus had to describe a condition in which 'rights and laws cover impious plans and judges sit on the bench deceitfully pretending to the impartiality of a Cato or a Cassius, but all cases are decided according to the will of a puffed-up power and by its whim the issue of life and death is decided for those who fall foul of it'.[57] Examples of the perversion of justice by the cruelty or insecurity of the emperor or the ambition of his ministers abound in Ammianus' *History*. We may here take his strictures on Valens, since they also illustrate once again the historian's attitude towards the imperial power. Ammianus admitted that Valens was justified in taking every precaution to preserve his life from traitors who were trying to kill him. But what was inexcusable was that Valens, swelling like a tyrant, was quick to oppress innocent and guilty alike without distinction of their deserts. Even while there was still doubt as to whether a crime had been committed at all, the emperor had decided on the penalty and men learned that they had been condemned before they knew they were under suspicion. His intolerable anger and tyrannical arrogance left him open to the intrigues and flattery of his courtiers.[58] The result was a reign of terror. Although the judges paraded the provisions of the law, they decided the cases according to the wish of their master who had completely abandoned the path of justice and equity. Judgement was given not on the basis of truth or the facts but according to the nod of one man.[59] In the end Valens' courtiers and ministers persuaded him to give up the administration of justice. It is interesting and significant that Ammianus, though he judged Valens a bloodthirsty tyrant, did not trouble to conceal his disapproval. This disapproval rested on two grounds. Firstly, it was the duty of an emperor to restrain the excesses of his subordinates and by leaving them in sole charge of the courts Valens gave free rein to their avarice and licence. Secondly, whether the emperor was just or unjust, the administration of the law was by virtue of his office one of his most important functions and to attempt to remove it from his power was a derogation of the imperial majesty.[60] Despite the rhetorical and emotional invocations of a personified Justice which occur regularly throughout Ammianus' work, he had a clear idea of what he meant by justice in the context of the Roman state. He did not mean a weak clemency or misplaced mercy. Justice stood for the strict letter of the law, the proper procedures of the courts and decisions reached on the basis of truth and the facts of the case, not by the cruelty or weakness of the emperor, the bias or avarice of the judges, the intrigues or ambitions of the courtiers. The strict letter of the law in the fourth century was frequently appallingly savage. But Ammianus supported it. As we have seen, he recognized Valens' right to defend himself by every legitimate means. Writing of the crime of treason, for which the procedures were the most savage of all, he said that no one with any sense would find fault if investigations into such matters were conducted more strictly than usual. All men ought to protect the safety of the emperor and in order that his safety might more strongly be protected, the laws exempted no one, high or low, from the most bloody interrogation under torture, when it was a question of repelling an attack upon the imperial majesty.[61] If a man was truly guilty then the law must take its course with all its rigour. Ammianus referred with approval to the actions of Theodosius who, in the course of suppressing the revolt of the Moor Firmus, burned alive Evasius and his son Florus and 'others who were clearly and openly convicted of having given aid to the disturber of the peace by secret counsel'.[62]

The concentration of immense power in the person of the emperor and the savagely repressive nature of the laws were alike dictated by the overriding necessity of the age, to preserve *Romania* from destruction by the barbarians who surrounded it. Above all, the emperor must be a soldier and not merely a strategist directing operations from a base in the rear of the armies, but an actual warrior facing the enemy direct and at close quarters. The defence of the empire took precedence over all else. Ultimately there was only one law: to defend the safety of the *respublica* against the barbarian invasions by every means and with the utmost vigour.[63] A vigorous defence of the imperial frontiers went far, to Ammianus' mind, to redeem other faults. Valentinian I is stigmatized as savagely cruel and as injuring the public good by excessively favouring the military.[64] Yet Ammianus remarked that no one, not even a persevering slanderer, would find fault with his unremitting care for the *respublica* if he considered that it was more useful to restrain the barbarians by proper frontier defences than to throw them back in battle.[65] Even Valens, whom Ammianus considered mad and rotten with stupidity, received praise from the historian for his steadfastness in the face of the demands of Sapor.[66] Valentinian's charge to Gratian on the latter's appointment as Augustus summarizes the position clearly: 'Gird yourself therefore for the tasks that press us hard as colleague of your father and uncle. Accustom yourself fearlessly to penetrate with the columns of infantry the Danube and the Rhine and cross with them on the ice, to stand close to your soldiers, to shed with full deliberation your blood and life for those whom you rule, to think nothing alien which pertains to the condition of the Roman empire.'[67] Over the centuries Ammianus and Valentinian join hands with Ennius and Decius Mus.[68]

One function of the speeches in Ammianus' *History* was clearly to present in dramatic form the author's concept of the nature of the state and the duties of public service. Thus Constantius to Julian: 'You have received in your prime, my brother, most beloved of all men, the splendid flower of your origin. My own glory is increased, I confess, since I consider myself more justly sublime in conferring almost equal power on a noble relative than in the power itself. Stand by me as a partner in labours and perils and receive the protection of the administration of Gaul of which you will relieve the afflicted parts with every assistance. And if it is necessary to meet the enemy, with firm step take your place among the standard-bearers themselves, with due deliberation encouraging daring at the right time, inspiring the fighting men by taking the lead with great caution, supporting those thrown into confusion with reinforcements, rebuking the cowards with moderation, as a most truthful witness stand by the energetic and the idle. Therefore at the urging of the greatness of the crisis, go forth as a brave man who is to lead men equally brave. We shall stand by each other in the strong steadfastness of mutual love, we will fight at the same time, together, if god wishes what we pray for, to rule a pacified world with equal self-control and dutifulness.'[69] This was the path to glory, as Julian said to his soldiers: 'By the decision of the god of heaven, I, mixing with you from my earliest youth, shattered the continual invasions of the Alamanni and the Franks and their lust for plunder and by your vigour and mine I made the Rhine crossable by the Roman armies as often as I wished, standing firm against the noise of rumour and the violent irruptions of strong tribes and relying on the sure foundation of your *virtus*. These labours Gaul which has seen them and which lives again after many deaths and long and bitter losses will commend to posterity through the swarms of the ages to come.'[70] Again and again in thus presenting his ideal, Ammianus expressed himself in the consecrated formulae of the old Roman tradition.

It is Julian whom Ammianus presents, not uncritically, as the nearly perfect embodiment of his ideal. In Julian justice, self-control and military ability were present to the highest degree.[71] His concern for the *respublica* overrode all else.[72] The result was that stability was secured within and without the frontiers of the empire, for the barbarians obeyed through fear and the *Romani* through love of the emperor.[73] 'On him ruling the Roman world in peace Fortune, as though bearing in her propitiousness an earthly cornucopia, bestowed everything glorious and prosperous, adding this also to the past records of his victories that while he held sole power, he was agitated by no internal revolts and none of the barbarians leaped across the frontiers. All the peoples, putting aside their greed for continual attacks as ruinous and harmful, were kindled to praise him with wonderful eagerness.'[74] Alone of all the emperors whose reigns Ammianus treats Julian was a man of *virtus*. Explicitly the historian compared him with the great heroes of the Republic. Before the invasion of Persia, Julian addressed his troops: 'If changeable fortune overcomes me in battle in any place, it will be sufficient for me to have given myself for the Roman world like the Curtii and Mucii of old and the glorious line of the Decii.'[75] On the site of Julian's tomb Ammianus asserts 'if anyone at the time had decided justly, the Cydnus ought not to look on his remains and ashes, although the river is very pleasant and limpid, but to perpetuate the glory of his noble deeds the Tiber, which divides the eternal city and washes the monuments of the ancient heroes, ought to flow by them'.[76] Immortal *gloria* won by great deeds in the service of the *respublica* and by high standards of morality, that is the sum of Julian's *virtus*. But to it Ammianus added the feature which traditionally distinguished the truly heroic from the merely great man. The great exploits which Julian performed in Gaul by his *virtus* and his *felicitas* surpassed many brave deeds of the men of old.[77] Like Rome herself, Julian combined with *virtus* the special favour of the gods manifested through the attentions of Fortune, which is what *felicitas* denoted.

Virtus was not for Ammianus specifically an imperial attribute. It lay open to anyone who performed gloriously in the service of the state. Ammianus saw that ministers and generals, civilians and soldiers were inextricably bound with the emperor in a nexus of obligation. Weakness anywhere was likely to start a reactive process which would end by endangering the stability and integrity of the whole empire. The ambition and malice of certain officials feeding with lying tales the ever alert suspicions of Constantius drove Silvanus to revolt as the only means of protecting himself.[78] Julian was compelled to acquiesce in, if not to engineer, the rising of his army by his knowledge of the same emperor's cruelty to his half-brother, Gallus.[79] The savagery of Valens gave rein to the avarice of his father-in-law Petronius which created the conditions for the revolt of Procopius.[80] The carelessness of Valentinian allowed Romanus and Palladius to ravage North Africa with impunity. Romanus further formed a homosexual attachment to the Moor Zammac and when his beloved was murdered by Firmus, exerted himself at court to destroy Firmus. He, fearing that he would be summarily executed, revolted from the empire.[81] Again and again in this way Ammianus insisted on the damage to the *respublica* that ensued when the vices of officials or courtiers fed or were fed by the vices of the emperor. The final disaster of his narrative, the battle of Adrianople, was provoked by a whole chain of moral deficiencies on the Roman side. When the Theruingian Goths appeared on the Danube in 376, experienced flatterers extolled the good fortune of Valens which had brought so many new recruits from the most distant lands. If he added them to his own and foreign troops, they said, he would have an invincible army. Further, the annual levy from the provinces could be abolished and the provincials made instead to pay monetary tribute, which would bring in a vast amount of gold to the treasury. Ammianus elsewhere condemns the habit of the provincials of paying gold to escape military service as frequently damaging to the state.[82] The flatterers so persuaded Valens that extreme care was exerted to ensure that no potential destroyer of the Roman state was left on the other side of the Danube.[83] The ruin of the Roman world having thus been admitted within the frontiers, the second fatal step was taken with the appointment to command in Thrace of two men of corrupt reputation, rivals in foolhardiness, Lupicinus and Maximus. It was their treacherous avarice, says Ammianus, which was the raw material of all the disasters. Both Lupicinus and Maximus and, with their connivance, their subordinates criminally exploited the Goths who were as yet innocent of any faults. Ammianus gives an example, which, as he says, no excuse could justify, not even if those responsible were judges of their own crimes. When the barbarians had crossed the river and were hard pressed by famine, Lupicinus and Maximus excogitated a disgusting traffic. They scoured the countryside for dogs, and exchanged them with the Goths for food at the rate of one dog for one slave.[84] Starved and exploited, the Theruingi put themselves under the leadership of Alavivus and Fritigern. Whereupon Lupicinus invited Alavivus and Fritigern to dinner and when the main body of the barbarians demonstrated for food he had the attendants of the two leaders killed. Ammianus adds a damning note on Lupicinus' condition: he had long been reclining at a sumptuous banquet with noisy entertainment and was drunk and sleepy. The result was the revolt of the Theruingi.[85] The annihilation of the Roman army came because of the pride of Valens himself. Supported by flattering courtiers he was eager to prevent Gratian from sharing a victory which, the flatterers insisted, was already won.[86]

Men and their characters determined the course of history for Ammianus, as for all Roman writers, not merely the historians, though in their works the attitude appears most clearly. For Ammianus it was not merely that moral deficiencies in the governors reduced the efficiency of government and the safety and stability of the state, but also that the fortunes of the *respublica* and its power, its strength or weakness, its rise or decline were inexorably determined by the moral health of its citizens. It has been fashionable to speak of the decline of the Roman empire in the west. Rather the process was less one of decline than one of change to a radically altered society. The reasons for the change are still imperfectly ascertained and imperfectly understood. Many of them may well be now beyond discovery. But among them we may mention the barbarian pressure on the frontiers set in motion by far-distant population movements, profound alteration of the economic structure of the empire which stemmed from the collapse of government and the invasions of the third century, the decline in urban culture and the progressive rise of the fortified manor with its peasants tied to the land. Ammianus, writing on the threshold of the emergence of mediaeval society, was but dimly aware of these and other factors. Although all three of the processes mentioned above are amply documented in his *History*, they remained for him largely isolated phenomena. Yet for all his, to us, incredible optimism as to the future, Ammianus could not escape the evidence of contemporary political decline. But when he attempted to account for this decline, he saw only psychological causes, specifically a decline in private morality. Writing in his summary of previous Roman disasters at the hands of foreign nations, which he prefixed to his description of the battle of Adrianople, of the times of Marcus Aurelius he said, 'But after calamitous disasters the state was soon restored, for this reason, because the ancient sobriety was not yet infected by the softness of a more dissolute way of life and did not gape after extravagant banquets or criminal gains, but high and low agreed with each other in unanimous ardour and hastened to a glorious death for the *respublica* as to some calm and peaceful harbour.'[87] Just so had Cato the Censor and Scipio Aemilianus, Sallust and Livy, or, rather, the annalists used by Livy, analysed the much less profound changes in their society. It is in connection with this belief that we must take the set-pieces in which Ammianus described the corruption of the contemporary city of Rome. What he has to say about the vices of the plebs need not detain us.[88] The existence of an idle and unemployed proletariate had been a major problem to the capital since at least the later second century BC. Rome was a magnet to men from Italy and the provinces. In a non-industrial society which made great use of slave labour many of these in-comers were not merely unemployed but unemployable. Rome not only had a non-industrial economy, but from the late second century BC to at least the early third century AD she had an increasingly sophisticated one. Sophisticated economies are not the best employers of labour. Full employment or any semblance of it can be maintained only in a comparatively backward economy whether industrialized or not. At Rome public works could provide temporary employment, transportation to colonies in Italy or overseas a temporary alleviation, but neither did anything to check the flow of immigrants. The doles introduced by C. Gracchus and repeated by later demagogues were condemned in ancient as in modern times. It is difficult to see an alternative. To exploit a public need for private advantage is a politician's function in any age. Sometimes a real need is thus identified and, more occasionally, met. By Ammianus' day Rome was no longer the centre of power, but largely decorative, a kept city. His remarks on the plebs are traditional in tone. From all we know they are likely to be true.

With his description of the vices of the nobility matters stand a little differently.[89] An inattentive reader might easily and forgivably suppose that he was reading a root and branch condemnation of the frivolity of the whole senatorial order. For, although at the beginning of his first excursus on the subject Ammianus says that the general splendour of Rome was harmed by 'the uncouth frivolity of a few',[90] in what follows this distinction is forgotten and the second disquisition is introduced as being concerned with the faults of the nobility and plebs without any distinction of a virtuous majority.[91] Further, Ammianus' handling of the specific charges in the first excursus belie his original reservation. On a number of occasions he explicitly claims to be describing the rule, not the exception.[92] There is ample evidence in the letters of Symmachus to prove Ammianus' picture a caricature. But it is a very traditional caricature in both subject and treatment. With the exceptions of the description of the eunuchs in the retinues of the great (it is debatable which Ammianus loathed more, eunuchs or elephants) and the personal tone of his castigation of the nobles for their arrogant neglect of worthy foreigners, there is nothing that could not have been written by the moralizing critics of the nobility in the Republic. Ostentation exhibiting itself in statues, carriages, luxurious and outlandish clothes, expensive and sumptuous banquets; frivolity shown in music and dancing; exclusive and intolerable arrogance; feminine debauchery and the avoidance of child-birth—these are the very faults lashed by men like Cato and Sallust and attacked in the long and ineffective tale of moral and sumptuary legislation in the Roman Republic. Of this tradition Ammianus was explicitly aware: such men did not know 'that their ancestors, by whom the greatness of Rome was extended so far, shone forth not by riches but through the fiercest wars, that neither in wealth nor way of life nor usefulness of dress did they differ from the common soldiers, that they conquered all obstacles by *virtus*'.[93] Once the nature of Ammianus' caricature is recognized, its purpose may be deduced. In the old Roman tradition of public service, which Ammianus fully accepted, terms such as frivolity and idleness tended to denote non-involvement in politics, all other activities being conceived as trivial beside the duty of a senator to take his part in public life. The letters of Symmachus disclose a society which, serious as it may have been about culture, was quite uninterested in public affairs except as they directly affected itself and its comfort. Further, Ammianus had a highly idealized view of the city of Rome and her function. It was not merely that the discovery that the Roman aristocracy fell far short of his ideal prompted him to harsh rebuke. Rome is described as the Lar of empire and *virtutes*.[94] By the word Lar he seems to mean that Rome performed in her empire the same function as the household god, the deified ancestor in a home. She was the tutelar deity who preserved the integrity of the whole. For Ammianus, as for the Romans for many centuries before him empire and *virtutes* were intimately connected. The state of the empire was determined by the *virtutes* of the citizens, especially of the leading men. Corruption and frivolity at the spiritual if no longer governmental centre had a direct relationship, causative rather than symptomatic (although the Roman tradition never made the distinction explicit), to the decline of the whole empire.

To move from Cicero and Sallust to Ammianus is, apparently, to move into a different world. The reader who makes the journey will notice, among much that is unfamiliar, Ammianus' total acceptance of the imperial system as reorganized by Diocletian and Constantine and, at the same time, his insistence that this system was merely a re-presentation of the *respublica* which stretched back to the foundation of the city. This sense of the continuity of Roman history was not a matter of superficial rhetorical embellishment by stock examples drawn from the past. Ammianus' involvement with Rome's past and its tradition formed the basis for his judgement of the present and its needs. Cato the Censor, if by an impossible fantasy he had read Ammianus' *History*, would have reacted to the events recorded with horror and disbelief. One thing he would have recognized instantly and approved: the standards by which Ammianus judged men and events and his view of the historical process and of the sources of strength and weakness in the Roman state.

CHAPTER VI

EPILOGUE

'It was through the Roman empire, so widely extended and so long lasting and so famous and glorious for the virtutes *of so great men, that the efforts of these men received the reward which they sought and for us examples have been put forward to remind us of our duty so that we may be pricked with shame if we for the most glorious city of God do not hold fast to the* virtutes *which are similar to those which they clung to for the sake of the glory of an earthly city.'*[1]

TO AMMIANUS Rome was the eternal city, destined to endure as long as the human race. Yet in AD 410, when Ammianus might still have been alive, although in extreme old age, Alaric the Visigoth captured and sacked the city.[2] The shock of horror which ran through the empire shows that Ammianus' description of Rome was no empty formula. Christians and pagans alike seem firmly to have believed that when Rome fell, the world would end. 'The whole world has perished in a single city' lamented Jerome in Bethlehem.[3] After the disaster of Adrianople Ammianus had offered to the Romans the cold comfort of an essay in historical perspective by reminding them of the previous defeats they had suffered at the hands of the barbarians.[4] But in 394 Theodosius had established Christianity as the imperial religion by prohibiting the pagan rites and abolishing the pagan calendar. The sack of Rome by Alaric was widely seen as punishment for this abandonment of the old gods. The strength of the shock to Christian and pagan alike and of the pagan reaction is demonstrated by Augustine's *De Civitate Dei*, which was begun to reassure the Christians and confute the arguments of the pagans.

Although the sack of Rome provided the initial impetus to Augustine's great work, in the dozen years, from 413 to 426, that he spent on its composition it grew far beyond the original conception and purpose. As we have it, the *De Civitate Dei* is concerned not primarily with Rome but with two great divisions of all mankind and the angels, the *Civitas Dei* and the *Civitas terrena*. This notion Augustine had already worked out in its essentials well before 410 and the *De Catechizandis Rudibus* of about 405 provides a convenient summary: 'Thus two states (*civitates*), one of the wicked, the other of the holy, endure from the birth of the human race to the end of time. Now they are thoroughly mingled in body but separated in will, but at the day of judgement they will be separated (in body too). All men who love arrogance and temporal domination with empty vanity and presumptuous display and all spirits who love such things and seek their own glory in the subjection of men are bound together in one society; but even if they often fight with each other for these things, nevertheless by equal weight of lust they are hurled into the same abyss and are joined to each other by the likeness of their habits and deserts. And, again, all men and all spirits who seek in humility the glory of God and who follow him in piety belong to one society.' While Augustine conceived the angelic components of his two *civitates* as rigorously distinct, the human members were inextricably intermingled, until the last judgement, without regard to national boundaries or ethnic and linguistic differences.[5] In working out this religious, indeed mystical concept, Augustine drew heavily on social and political models and terminology.[6] The great model was, of course, the Roman empire. If in his completed work Augustine was not primarily concerned with Rome, it was from Rome and Roman definitions that he began.

Civitas, to take first the most obvious example, is twice formally defined. In the second book of the *De Civitate Dei*, with reference to the story of Regulus, we read '*civitas* is nothing other than a concordant multitude of men'.[7] This recalls Sallust's description of the foundation of Rome: 'In a short time a scattered and wandering multitude became a *civitas* through *concordia*.' Augustine, in fact, quotes this sentence in a letter in connection with another definition of *civitas*: 'What is a *civitas* except a multitude of men brought together in a sort of bond of *concordia*.'[8] This again is close to the second definition in the *De Civitate Dei*: 'Nor can a *civitas* consist in one person, since it is nothing other than a multitude of men bound together by some bond of association.'[9] That a *civitas* differed from a mere multitude or mob in possessing a common organization or unifying principle was a traditional Roman position, long a commonplace of political theory. But it was hardly a very precise definition. It was just this lack of precision which gave Augustine his opportunity. For having thus employed a traditional definition to establish the basic nature of his two *civitates* he then made explicit the unifying principle as 'love', *amor*: 'Two loves have made the two *civitates*; the *civitas terrena* is made by love of self even to contempt of God, the heavenly *civitas* by love of God even to contempt of self.'[10] Exactly how Augustine conceived the operation and effect of the two loves we are not here concerned to analyse. But we must notice that no Roman would have admitted love, of God or of anything else, as the chief unifying principle of the state. The Roman attitude was that the fundamental characteristic of the civilized state, which distinguished it equally from barbaric anarchy and tyranny and which secured and assured *concordia*, was justice and the rule of law. This, above all, was what *respublica* signified.[11] Of this Augustine was, of course, well aware. In his reply to those who blamed Rome's disasters on Christianity, he pointed out, with some justice, that Rome had suffered many disasters before Christ. Extensive quotation from Cicero's *De Republica* led him to a discussion of the nature of the *respublica*. Augustine accepted the Ciceronian definition that the *res publica* was the *res populi* and that a *populus* was a 'gathering united by common law and mutual advantage'. But just as he accepted the ancient definition of *civitas* only to turn it to his own purpose, so he disagreed with the application of Cicero's definition of *respublica* to Rome. Equating 'common law' (*iuris consensus*) with 'justice' (*iustitia*) he argued that *iustitia* is a theological virtue and that the Romans, being pagans, had never had a true *respublica* because, almost by definition, they could never have had true justice. 'True justice does not exist except in that *respublica* whose founder and ruler is Christ, if indeed we please to call it a *respublica* since we certainly cannot deny that it is *res populi*.'[12] Augustine returned to this point in greater detail in Book XIX where he took up the promise made in Book II to show from Scipio's definitions in Cicero's *De Republica* that the Roman *respublica* never truly existed.[13] Once again he began with the equation *res publica*=*res populi* and the definition of *populus* quoted above. He then continued: 'But what he means by common law he explains in argument, showing that a *respublica* cannot function without justice; where true justice does not exist, law cannot exist either.' Therefore where true justice does not exist, a gathering of men united by common law cannot exist and therefore a *populus* as defined by Scipio, or, rather, Cicero, cannot exist either. And if no *populus*, then no *res populi* and hence no *res publica*. Justice Augustine defined as 'a virtue which gives to each his own'. This is sufficiently close to Cicero's definition in the *De Finibus* of justice as 'an affection of the mind giving to each his own' to allow us to suppose that the Augustinian definition may have come from the *De Republica*.[14] But Augustine went on to ask 'What human justice is it that takes man himself from the true God and hands him over to unclean demons? Is this to give each his own?' Next Augustine brought up the justification of Roman imperialism as benefiting the subjects and showed Cicero supporting this justification by asking 'Why then does God rule men, the mind rule the body, reason rule lust and the other vicious parts of the mind?' To which Augustine rejoined 'Therefore, when a man does not serve God, what justice can be considered to be in him?' The Romans did not serve God. Therefore, if there was no justice in the individual, there was no justice in the collection of individuals. Thus, again, the Roman *respublica* did not exist. Again, with regard to the second component of Cicero's definition of the *populus*, mutual advantage, Augustine said: 'There is no advantage for living men, if they live impiously as every man lives who does not serve God but serves demons which are the more impious the more they wish sacrifice to be paid to themselves as though they were gods, although they are the most unclean spirits.'

Augustine's method is extremely interesting. Throughout his discussion of *civitas*, *populus* and *respublica* he started from the accepted and traditional Roman definitions. Then by importing a specifically theological consideration or by interpreting a key word in the original definition in a theological sense, he turned the definition back on the Romans' heads. It is important, however, to understand that Augustine was only incidentally concerned with polemic. His chief purpose was not to destroy the Roman tradition but to convert it and to use it as the foundation of his concept of the two *civitates* which formed the subject of his book. This becomes apparent if we pursue Augustine's argument about the nature of the *respublica* a little further.[15] Having refuted to his own satisfaction Cicero's definition of *populus* he advanced another: 'A *populus* is the gathering of a rational multitude' (*i.e.* of men, not beasts) 'united in the mutual communion of the things which it loves.' What Augustine has done is to replace justice, for him a positive theological virtue, with a morally indifferent unifying principle. Any group of men with any common interest may be considered a *populus*. The moral worth of any *populus* depends on the moral worth of its common interest. From this point of view, the old Roman *populus* was indeed a *populus*, but a bad one since its common interest was bad. But Augustine's object was not so much to condemn the *populus Romanus* or any other historical nation, but to construct a model definition of *populus* which would include both the *Civitas Dei* and the *Civitas terrena* or, at least, their human members.

It is noticeable that in this adaptation of traditional terminology of political organization, the more technical the term the greater was Augustine's difficulty. *Civitas* caused little trouble, *populus* required intensive discussion, with *respublica* Augustine was never wholly happy. He used it, in the majority of its occurrences, of the Roman state. When he wished to apply it to his main theme he replaced it by *populus*, by the equation *res publica = res populi* and then redefined *populus* to be as morally indifferent as *civitas*. On the rare occasions when he used *respublica* in direct reference to the *Civitas Dei*, he apologized for it.[16] What is important for our purpose is that Augustine in constructing his theological and mystical design of the human and angelic condition did not invent a new vocabulary, but turned naturally to the political and social terminology of Rome. This terminology he clearly recognized as still possessing considerable power and vitality; hence the violence of his redefinitions.

Augustine did not confine his attention to the pagan gods and the Roman terms for governmental and social organization. He met the charge that Rome's calamities were due to Christianity first by pointing out that Rome had suffered many miserable disasters before Christ and then by a direct attack on the pagan gods whom he represented as either impotent fictions or positively evil spirits.[17] But he could not deny the existence of the Roman empire and the benefits it had conferred. Since he believed that all things were ruled by the universal providence of God[18] and that the pagan gods, being either powerless or evil, could not have enlarged and preserved the Roman empire,[19] then the Romans too, although they worshipped false gods and obscene demons, owed their successes to almighty God.[20] The discussion of why this was so led Augustine to a lengthy treatment of the Roman ideal of *virtus*. It is significant that Augustine began the treatment with Sallust and drew heavily on him throughout this section. Sallust had not merely painted a picture of moral decline much to Augustine's taste and purpose, but of all Roman writers he had given the most extensive and direct discussion of the nature and effects of *virtus*. Beginning with a quotation from the *Bellum Catilinae* Augustine, supplementing and illustrating Sallust with quotations from Virgil's *Aeneid*, described at length and in a remarkably untendentious manner the ideal of *virtus* as the winning of *gloria* in the service of the state by great deeds and high moral standards.[21] The two points which most concerned Augustine were *gloria* and morality. Just as he attempted to demolish Cicero's definition of *respublica* by a shift in the meaning of *iustitia*, wholly illicit from the point of view of strict argumentation, so here, having described the Roman passion for *gloria*, he then attacked it from a theological standpoint as a vice. Cicero in the *De Republica* had asserted that the leader of the state (*princeps civitatis*) should be nourished by *gloria* and that his own ancestors had done many amazing and wonderful deeds because of their desire for *gloria*. 'Thus', Augustine continued, 'not only did they not resist this vice but they even thought it should be excited and kindled in the belief that it was useful to the *respublica*. Moreover, even in his books on philosophy Cicero did not avoid this plague, since in them he confesses it more clearly than the light of day.'[22] Augustine opposed the Roman notion of *gloria* because it implied love of man rather than of God. 'For this vice is so great an enemy of holy faith, if the desire of *gloria* is greater in a man's heart than the fear or love of God, that the Lord said "How can you believe when you expect *gloria* from each other and do not seek the *gloria* which is from God alone?" '[23] But, although the Romans, lacking true holiness, could not qualify for eternal life with the angels in heaven, their virtues (Augustine used the Sallustian expression *bonae artes*) had been such that God could not but reward them. Since the aim of their great deeds and moral qualities was glorification, God gave them the temporal reward: 'Thus they too despised private wealth for the common good, that is, for the *respublica*, and for its treasury, they resisted avarice, they consulted the interests of their native land with free deliberation, guilty according to their laws of neither crime nor lust; by all these practices they strove, as though by the true path, for offices, power and *gloria*. They were honoured in nearly all nations, they imposed the laws of their empire on many nations and today they are glorious in literature and history among almost all nations. There is no reason for them to complain of the justice of the highest and true God: "they have received their reward".'[24] Augustine's words, it will be apparent, are a fair and accurate summary of the aristocratic ideal of the Roman Republic and he judged it as not contemptible as earthly and pagan things go. Indeed, Augustine went further. The traditional heroes of Rome, men like Torquatus, Camillus, Mucius, Curtius, the Decii, Regulus, Cincinnatus, Fabricius could offer even to Christians examples of poverty, faith and contempt for temporal and material pleasure and advantage in devotion to a higher ideal.[25] Indeed the existence of these heroes was part of the divine purpose: 'The Roman empire was not extended to human glory merely that such a reward should be paid to such men, but also so that the citizens of that eternal city, as long as they are pilgrims here, should carefully and soberly gaze on those examples and see how great a love is owed to the heavenly land for the sake of eternal life if the earthly land was so much loved by its citizens for the sake of human *gloria*.'[26] Yet for all his concessions Augustine remained firm that even the noblest of the ancient Romans lacked the smallest qualification for salvation: 'Let it be agreed among all who are truly holy that no one can have true *virtus* without true holiness, that is the true worship of the true God, nor is that true *virtus* when it serves human *gloria*.'[27]

As in his discussions of the nature of the state, so with regard to *virtus* Augustine began with the ancient definition: *virtus* is the practice of living worthily and rightly.[28] This is an unexceptional statement which would include with equal facility the Roman ideal and the many special definitions of the philosophers—not that these two categories were by any means distinct and separate. The 'conversion' of the pagan philosophers caused Augustine little trouble, although he felt obliged to spend a considerable time on their views.[29] By a process of rejection, selection and reinterpretation he was able to turn to his own purpose the ethical and even the theological teachings of the pagan philosophers.[30] It was largely a matter of defining in a Christian sense the practice of living worthily and rightly and the felicity which attended *virtus*.[31] The Roman ideal he found more difficult. It was not merely that Augustine himself felt its force strongly, but that he was handling not the ideas of a single philosopher or even of a school of philosophy, which other philosophers and other schools might reject, but the tradition of a whole civilization in which he himself had been educated and which was supremely relevant to his concept of the two mystical *civitates*. The source of the difficulty, as so often in the past, was *gloria*. Augustine condemned the Roman ideal of *virtus* because it proposed as its aim temporal and human *gloria*. In the Christian scheme *gloria* belonged to God alone.[32] Before Augustine could accommodate the Roman tradition, this shift in meaning and emphasis had to be made. The heroes of Rome were replaced by the holy apostles.[33] They did not behave as the old Romans had done. 'When they preached the name of Christ in those places where it was not merely disapproved (as Cicero says, "those things which are disapproved by certain people always lie low") but even considered as an object of the greatest detestation, holding fast to what they had heard from the good master who is also the doctor of men's minds, "If anyone denies me before men, I will deny him before my father who is in heaven" or "before the angels of God", amid cursing and abuse, amid the most terrible persecutions and cruel punishments, they were not terrified by the great raging of human opposition from preaching the salvation of humanity. Although by performing divine deeds and speaking divine words and living in a divine way and by defeating in war, so to speak, the hard hearts of men and introducing the peace of justice they won enormous *gloria* in the church of God, they did not retire on that *gloria* as though it were the consummation of their *virtus*, but by referring that *gloria* also to the *gloria* of God, by whose grace they were as they were, with this tinder they inflamed those with whose interests they were concerned to the love of him who made them too such as they were.'[34] Nor was it merely in the actual church that this adaptation of the Roman ideal could operate, but in the mystic *civitas Dei* itself, when it attained eternal happiness and the rest of the everlasting Sabbath. 'There there will be true *gloria*, where no one will be praised through error or adulation of the praiser; true honour, which will be denied to no one who is worthy and conferred on no one who is unworthy nor will anyone who is unworthy canvass for it, where none will be admitted except the worthy; there will be true peace, where no one will suffer hostility either from himself or from anyone else. The reward of *virtus* will be He who gave *virtus* and promised himself, than whom nothing could be better and greater. What else was it that He spoke through the prophet, "I will be their God and they will be my people", than "I will be the source of their satisfaction, I will be whatever is honourably desired by men, life and safety, food and wealth, *gloria* and honour and peace and all good things?".... But what will be the grades of rewards, honours and glories in proportion to merit, who is fit to consider, much less to say? But that they will exist does not admit of argument.'[35] It is a very Roman heaven.

Thus Augustine succeeded in his adaptation of the Roman ideal to the service of the Christian church. In the end it proved not over difficult. Almost four centuries before Virgil had taken the essential step, for in the *Aeneid*, *gloria* attaches not to the individual but to the country and the mission. The hero by his great deeds glorifies not himself but his native land. Not that it is necessary or desirable to see a direct connection between Virgil and Augustine, for all the latter's tears over Dido. But the change which Augustine found essential was well within the vital versatility of the Roman tradition. Augustine was able to draw not merely on over six centuries of development of the Roman ideal but also on Scripture and the Fathers who preceded him. Words such as *virtus* and *gloria* had long established themselves in Christian theology. Nor was Augustine the first Christian to feel the force of the Roman ideal, though few had felt it as powerfully relevant as he. But in the *De Civitate Dei* the speculations of the pagan philosophers and the moral and political tradition of Rome were fused with and transmuted by the teachings of the Scriptures and the doctrines of the early Fathers to serve the ideal of the Church and the glory of God.

Here we must leave the Roman ideal, safely embarked on a new career. Its later fortunes in the service of the Church and its efflorescence as a secular ideal in the Renaissance would themselves demand a large book. It was never a very profound or original idea. Imperfectly defined, it is hardly to be dignified with the name of thought. Rather it represented the unsystematic collection of attitudes, emotions and sentiments with which the Romans faced men and affairs. The very imprecision of the tradition was the source of its great strength. Romans of all sorts, not merely politicians and historians, operated in their judgement of events with a few simple, but deeply felt, moral concepts. Summed up in the idea of *virtus* they formed a tradition of remarkable strength and longevity. In the second century BC *virtus* expressed particularly the aristocratic ideal of personal pre-eminence won in the service of the state. In the Ciceronian age the new men opposed their idea of a personal and individual *virtus* giving birth to a personal and individual nobility to what they claimed was the perversion of the aristocratic ideal by the *nobiles*. Livy's *History*, at least as we have it, is a celebration of the aristocratic ideal, but Virgil and Horace, more thoughtful than he, reflect in their use of *virtus* and allied terms the destruction of the Republic by the ruinous ambition of the *nobiles* and the establishment of the Principate. Tacitus succeeded in reconciling the old tradition with the new conditions of the developed imperial system. Yet when, at the end of the fourth century AD, the Roman empire in the west, now a ferocious despotism propped up by a harshly repressive code of law, was crumbling before the onslaughts of the barbarians, the best analysis that Ammianus could offer was a moral one. Let Rome return to the good ways of the reign of Marcus Aurelius and all would be well. In his analysis of Roman corruption he joined hands over more than five centuries with Cato the Censor and Scipio Aemilianus. Nor was Ammianus alone. Writers as diverse as Claudian and Augustine turned back to Sallust who had most carefully treated the relationship between the breakdown of *virtus* and political decline—and they accepted his case. Against all experience the Romans, century after century, persisted in the belief that moral health and political power and stability were indissolubly joined, that men could be legislated into virtue. Banal and cliché-ridden though it may appear to us, it did not appear so to Ammianus and Augustine. For them the tradition was alive and very much to be reckoned with. A tradition which endured for the whole life of western Roman civilization and to which all Roman public writers felt themselves obliged to relate cannot be dismissed as unimportant. Close study of this tradition through its many adaptations and redefinitions can teach us much about the way in which the Roman mind worked and explain much about Roman actions and reactions. Not infrequently the nature of a society is most clearly revealed in its most cherished clichés.

NOTES

ABBREVIATIONS

B.C.	*Bellum Catilinae*
B.J.	*Bellum Iugurthinum*
C.A.H.	*Cambridge Ancient History*
CIL	*Corpus Inscriptionum Latinarum*
C.J.	*Classical Journal*
C.Q.	*Classical Quarterly*
C.Ph.	*Classical Philology*
HRR	H. Peter, *Historicorum Romanorum Reliquiae*, I, 2nd ed., 1914, II, 1906
ILS	H. Dessau, *Inscriptiones Latinae Selectae*, 1892–1916
J.R.S.	*Journal of Roman Studies*
MRR	T. R. S. Broughton, *The Magistrates of the Roman Republic*, American Philological Association, 1951–2
ORF[2]	H. Malcovati, *Oratorum Romanorum Fragmenta Liberae Reipublicae*, 2nd ed., 1955
P.A.C.A.	*Proceedings of the African Classical Associations*
P.B.S.R.	*Papers of the British School at Rome*
Phil.	*Philologus*
P-W	Pauly-Wissowa-Kroll, *Real Encyclopaedie der classischen Altertumswissenschaft*
R.E.L.	*Revue des Etudes Latines*
ROL	E. Warmington, *Remains of Old Latin*, Loeb Classical Library, vols. I–III, 1935–38
T.A.P.A.	*Transactions of the American Philological Asssciation*

CHAPTER I

1 Macrobius III, 13, 19: 'gravissimus alienae luxuriae obiurgator et censor'
2 For an illustration of how far the Patriciate had declined by the second century BC see the reconstruction of the Senate of 179 in P. Willems, *Le*

Sénat de la république romaine, I (1878), 303ff. On the concept of *nobilitas* see M. Gelzer, *Die Nobilität der römischen Republik* (1912) and A. Afzelius, *Class. et Med.* 1945, 198ff

3 As, for instance, Sallust's remarks in *B.C.* 23, 6 and *B.J.* 63, 7 that the *nobiles* considered the consulship polluted if held by a new man, *cf.* D. C. Earl, *Historia*, 1966, 302ff; E. Badian, *Gnomon*, 1964, 384; *Durham University Journal*, 1964, 141ff

4 *E.g.* Cicero, *In Pis.* 1; Tacitus, *Ann.* III, 17; *Hist.* IV, 11. On the Calpurnii Pisones in the second century see D. C. Earl, *Athenaeum*, 1960, 283ff

5 *E.g.* Cicero, *De Nat. Deorum* III, 11. On Cato see further above, pp. 44ff

6 *Cf.* D. C. Earl, *Latomus*, 1960, 658

7 Cicero, *De Amicitia*, 71

8 H. H. Scullard, *Roman Politics 220–150 B.C.* (1951), 12ff; G. De Sanctis, *Storia dei Romani*, IV, i (1923), 489ff; Th. Mommsen, *Römische Forschungen*, I (1864), 321ff; A. von Premerstein, *P-W* IV, 23ff

9 E. Badian, *Foreign Clientelae (264–70 B.C.)* (1958)

10 *Cf.* A. H. M. Jones, *Studies in Roman Government and Law* (1960), 3f

11 See H. H. Scullard, *Roman Politics*, 8ff; R. Syme, *The Roman Revolution* (1939), 8ff; M. Gelzer, *Nobilität*, 50ff

12 Livy XXXIX, 6, 7. On the tradition of the moral crisis generally see D. C. Earl, *The Political Thought of Sallust* (1961), 41ff

13 *Cf.* C. O. Brink and F. W. Walbank, *C.Q.* 1954, 103ff

14 Polybius XXXI, 25, 3ff; *cf.* Diodorus XXXI, 26; Polybius VI, 57, 5

15 Pliny *N.H.* XVII, 244=Piso fr. 38, *HRR*; *cf.* Festus p. 285 (Lindsay). On the censors of 154 BC see Valerius Maximus II, 4, 2; Livy XLIII, 1, 4ff. They proposed the building of a permanent theatre but were prevented by P. Cornelius Scipio Nasica on the grounds that such construction was useless and harmful to public morals, Livy, *Periocha* XLVIII; *cf.* Valerius Maximus II, 4, 2; Velleius Paterculus I, 15, 3. On this year see also Livy, *Periocha* XLVII; Valerius Maximus VI, 9, 10; Festus, p. 360 (Lindsay); Livy, *Periocha* XLVIII

16 Polybius XXXII, 13, 6

17 Florus I, 31, 5; Appian, *Lib.* 69; Plutarch, *Cato Maior* 27; Diodorus XXXIV 33, 3–6. *Cf.* E. Bikerman, *REL*, 1946, 150; A. Aymard, *Mélanges de la societé toulousaine d'études classiques* 1948, 109, note 12; H. H. Scullard, *Roman Politics*, 241ff; D. C. Earl, *The Political Thought of Sallust*, 47f

18 Sallust, *B.C.* 10, 1ff; *cf. B.J.* 41, 1; *Hist.* fr. 11; 12, M; *cf.* Pliny *N.H.* XXXIII, 150; Velleius Paterculus II, 1, 1; Florus I, 33, 1; 34, 18; 47, 2; Augustine, *De Civitate Dei* I, 30; Orosius V, 8, 2. The year 146 BC also marked an epoch in popular thought in the provinces, see A. N. Sherwin-White, *The Roman Citizenship* (1939) 234ff

19 Sallust, *B.C.* 11, 5–8

20 The clearest example of the social attitude of the Roman nobility to politics

is found in the use of the word 'amicitia', 'friendship', to denote not a sentimental tie based on congeniality, but political alliance and faction based on common interest, *cf. e.g.* Sallust, *B.C.* 20, 4: nam idem velle atque idem nolle ea demum firma amicitia est; *B.J.* 31, 15: eadem cupere, eadem odisse, eadem metuere . . . haec inter bonos amicitia, inter malos factio est. *Cf.* R. Syme, *Roman Revolution*, 12; 157

21 On what follows see R. E. Smith, *The Aristocratic Epoch in Latin Literature* (1947); D. C. Earl, *The Political Thought of Sallust*, Chapter II

22 Cicero, *Tusc. Disp.* II, 18, 43; A. Ernout and A. Meillet, *Dictionnaire Etymologique de la langue latine*, *s.v.* 'vir'; A. Ernout, *Philologica Classica* (1946), 225ff. For a different, dynamic interpretation see A. N. van Omme, *Virtus, een semantiese studie*, Diss. Utrecht, 3ff

23 *CIL* I^2 9: 'Honc oino ploirume cosentiont Romane/duonoro optumo fuise viro'. He was consul in 259, censor in 258 BC. *Cf. MRR* I, 206; Tenney Frank, *C.Q.* 1921, 169ff

24 Cicero, *De Senectute* 61: 'Hunc unum plurimae consentiunt gentes/populi primarium fuisse virum'

25 See, for instance, the pontifical and augural colleges of 210 BC as reconstructed in *MRR* I, 282f

26 *Cf.* Cicero, *De Legibus* II, 12, 30f

27 See the sources referred to in D. C. Earl, *The Political Thought of Sallust*, 20, note 3

28 Polybius VI, 56, 6f. On religion and politics generally see Th. Mommsen, *Römisches Staatsrecht* I^3 (1887), 76; L. R. Taylor, *Party Politics in the Age of Caesar* (1949), Chapter IV

29 *CIL* I^2 7. Barbatus was consul in 298, censor, perhaps, in 280 BC. See *MRR* I, 174; 191

30 'Fortis vir sapiensque' *Cf.* Ennius, *Annales* fr. 271 *ROL* I: 'Qualis consiliis quantumque potesset in armis'; 396: 'Primus senex bradys in regimen belloque peritus'

31 *CIL* I^2 10: 'honos fama virtusque gloria atque ingenium'

32 *CIL* I^2 11: 'ne quairatis honore quei minus sit mandatus'

33 *The Aristocratic Epoch in Latin Literature*, 10

34 Sallust, *B.C.* 4; *B.J.* 4, 3ff. *Cf.* R. Syme, *Sallust* (1964), 43ff; D. C. Earl, *J.R.S.* 1965, 234

35 Pliny, *N.H.* VII, 139

36 *Cf.* Livy XXXIX, 40 on Cato the Censor

37 Ennius *Annales* fr. 200–2 (*cf.* Cicero, *Tusc. Disp.* I, 39, 69; *De Finibus* II, 19, 16; Cato *Origines* fr. 83 *HRR*); 378–9; 360–2; *cf.* 549; 393–4; 131; *Inc. Sed.* 31 *ROL I*

38 Ennius, *Annales* fr. 210–27 *ROL* I

39 See D. C. Earl, *Historia*, 1960, 235ff

40 Plautus, *Stichus* 280ff: Propera, Pinacium, pedes hortare, honesta dicta

factis/—nunc tibi potestas adipiscendist gloriam laudem decus/—eraeque egenti subveni—benefacta maiorum tuom

41 Plautus, *Curculio* 284ff; *cf. Trinummus* 272ff; 655ff. The positions mentioned are, of course, Greek and the passage must be seen in the context of the traditional Roman attitude to things Greek, which is discussed on pp. 36ff of the text

42 *Cf.* D. C. Earl, *Historia*, 1960, 235f

43 Plautus, *Trinummus*, 642ff

44 Polybius XXXI, 23. See further on Scipio above pp. 36ff

45 Polybius VI, 53f; O. C. Crawford, *C.J.* 1941, 17ff

46 *CIL* I^2, 15

47 *Cf.* D. C. Earl, *Tiberius Gracchus: A Study in Politics* (1963), 107ff

48 See H. H. Scullard, *J.R.S.* 1960, 70f; L. R. Taylor, *J.R.S.* 1962, 1ff; D. C. Earl, *Tiberius Gracchus*, 46f; 76f; 108f

49 Ennius, *Annales* fr. 467 *ROL* I; Cicero, *De Republica* V, 1ff. *Cf.* H. Roloff, *Maiores bei Cicero* (1938); E. Lepore, *Il Princeps Ciceroniano* (1954), 218ff; D. C. Earl, *The Political Thought of Sallust*, 25; *Historia*, 1960, 237

50 On colonization in Italy see E. Badian, *Foreign Clientelae* 162f; on the enfranchisement of the Italians, *ibid.* chapters VIII to X

51 See D. C. Earl, *Tiberius Gracchus*, passim

52 D. C. Earl, *Historia*, 1960, 239f

53 Cicero, *Pro Sestio*, 139; *Phil.* I, 29; *cf. Tusc. Disp.* III, 2, 3

54 See the passages from Ennius and Plautus quoted above and D. C. Earl, *Historia*, 1960, 236; 239f

55 Ennius, *Annales* fr. 186–93; *ROL* I

56 Cicero, *In Verrem* II, ii, 122; *Parad.* IV, 43f; Livy XXI, 63, 4; XXII, 25f; Valerius Maximus III, 4, 4; *cf.* Cicero, *De Officiis* I, 150f

57 Cicero, *De Republica* IV, 7, 7; *Brutus* 232; Valerius Maximus III, 4, 2; *cf.* Piso fr. 11; 62; 87 *HRR*; Dionysius Hal. IX, 25

58 On *dignitas* see H. Wegehaupt, *Die Bedeutung und Anwendung von Dignitas in den Schriften der republikanischen Zeit*, Diss. Breslau (1932); R. Syme, *Roman Revolution*, 13 and passim

59 *Cf.* Cato, *De Agricultura*, proem; Cicero, *De Officiis* I, 150f. H. Hill, *The Roman Middle Class* (1952), 48; 50. On the relations of *equites* and *nobiles cf.* R. Syme, *Roman Revolution*, 13ff; 151

60 Ennius, *Annales* fr. 209 *ROL* I

61 *Cf.* Plautus, *Captivi* 690; 683–9; D. C. Earl, *Historia* 1960, 240

62 Claudius Quadrigarius fr. 41 *HRR*. See below pp. 76ff on Livy

63 Ennius, *Annales* fr. 333–5; 434–5; *cf.* 405 *ROL* I

64 Plautus, *Amphitruo* 75–8. *Cf.* D. C. Earl, *The Political Thought of Sallust*, 24; *Historia*, 1960, 240f

65 Plautus, *Menaechmi* 571ff

66 Cicero, *De Officiis* I, 7; *Bell. Hisp.* 19, 6. On *fides* generally see E. Badian,

Foreign Clientelae, 1ff and the discussions there referred to; *cf.* Dionysius Hal. II, 9–11; E. Gabba, *Athenaeum* 1960, 175ff

67 Plautus, *Cistellaria* 197ff

68 E. Badian, *Foreign Clientelae*, 4ff

69 On *auctoritas* see R. Syme, *Roman Revolution*, 10; 152f; *Tacitus*, 412f and the discussions there referred to. A useful collection of the passages in Republican authors dealing with the political vocabulary will be found, with extensive bibliography, in J. Hellegouarc'h, *Le Vocabulaire Latin des Relations et des Partis Politiques sous la Republique* (1963)

70 Plautus, *Truculentus* 493ff

71 *Cf.* Ennius *Annales* fr. 262–8 *ROL* I

72 Plautus, *Miles Gloriosus* 11f; *cf.* 31f; 1027; *Epidicus* 444ff; *Pseudolus* 531; *Curculio* 178 ff

73 Plautus, *Asinaria* 558f; *Miles Gloriosus* 649

74 *Cf.* D. C. Earl, *Historia*, 1962, 474ff

75 *Cf.* D. C. Earl, *The Political Thought of Sallust* 26f; *Historia* 1962, 482

76 *E.g.* A. Schmekel, *Die Philosophie der mittleren Stoa* (1892), especially 439ff

77 On what follows see D. C. Earl, *Historia* 1962, 477ff; F. W. Walbank, *J.R.S.* 1965, 1ff

78 Valerius Maximus VI, 4, 2, *cf.* Auct. Vir. Ill, 58, 9

79 A. Gellius *N.A.* VI, 20, 1=Scipio fr. 13 *ORF²*. Gellius calls the speech 'oratio quam dixit in censura cum ad maiorum mores populum hortaretur' and 'oratio . . . quam censor habuit ad populum de moribus', V, 19, 15= Scipio fr. 14 *ORF²*

80 Scipio fr. 17–26; 30 *ORF²*

81 *E.g.* cinaedus, psalterio, crotalis, sambuca, chiridota, Scipio fr. 30 and 17 *ORF²* Compare Lucilius' use of Greek words in similar contexts, *e.g.* fr. 13; 15; 60; 277; 1048 *ROL* III. Especially compare Lucilius fr. 33 *ROL* III: 'stulte saltatum te inter veniise cinaedos', with Scipio fr. 30 *ORF²*: 'eunt, inquam, in ludum saltatorium inter cinaedos virgines puerique ingenui'

82 Polybius XXXI, 25ff. See above pp. 26f

83 From the funeral laudation of Aemilianus written by C. Laelius for delivery by Q. Fabius Maximus, Laelius fr. 23=Fabius fr. 3 *ORF²*. On Scipio as a politician see A. Aymard, *Mélanges de la societe toulousaine d'études classiques* 1948, 101ff; K. Bilz, *Die Politik des P. Cornelius Scipio Aemilianus* (1935); C. O. Brink and F. W. Walbank, *C.Q.* 1954, 104; M. Gelzer, *Vom römischen Staat* I (1943), 111ff; H. H. Scullard, *J.R.S.* 1960, 59ff; A. E. Astin, *Latomus* 1956, 159ff

84 Cicero, *De Republica* I, 34; 36; III, 5; *De Oratore* II, 154; *Topica*, 78; *Pro Archia* 16; *cf.* Velleius Paterculus I, 13, 3. Compare Cicero, *De Natura Deorum* III, 5: 'But on matters of religion I follow Ti. Coruncanius, P. Scipio, P. Scaevola the *pontifices maximi*, not Zeno or Cleanthes or

Chrysippus. I hold fast to C. Laelius, an augur and a wise man, to whom I would rather listen speaking about religion in that famous and noble speech than any of the leaders of the Stoics.' In 145 BC C. Laelius as praetor and augur successfully opposed the proposal of the tribune C. Licinius Crassus that the priesthoods should be filled by popular election, see Cicero, *De Natura Deorum* III, 43; *De Amicitia* 96; *Phil.* II, 83; Laelius fr. 12–16 *ORF*[2]

85 Some senators in the second century BC reached a high pitch of expertise in Greek. Besides Q. Fabius Pictor and C. Acilius who wrote histories of Rome in Greek, note, *e.g.* Ti. Sempronius Gracchus, who greatly impressed the faculty at the university of Rhodes with his rhetorical ability, and P. Licinius Crassus Mucianus, consul in 131 BC, who was fluent in five Greek dialects. By 167 BC Greek *grammatici* were teaching at Rome: Polybius XXXI, 24. It was a hazardous profession, however. In 161 all philosophers and rhetors were banished from Rome by the Senate

86 Plutarch, *Cato Maior* 22, 5

87 *Cf.* W. Capelle, *Klio* 1932, 86ff; D. C. Earl, *Historia* 1962, 482f; F. W. Walbank, *J.R.S.* 1965, 13ff.; H. Strasburger, *J.R.S.* 1965, 40ff

88 Livy XXIX, 10, 4ff; 14, 5ff; Dionysius Hal. II, 19, 5

89 Livy XXXIX, 8ff; A. H. McDonald, *J.R.S.* 1944, 27ff; D. C. Earl, *Historia*, 1962, 484

90 Livy *Periocha*, XLVII

CHAPTER II

1 Cicero, *Ep. ad Hirt.* fr. 3, Purser

2 On Cato see D. Keinast, *Cato der Zensor* (1954); H. H. Scullard, *Roman Politics*, passim

3 Cornelius Nepos, *Cato* 3, *cf.* Pliny *N.H.* VIII, 11 = Cato *Origines* fr. 88 *HRR*. Cato's practice applied not only to Romans but to Rome's enemies, but not to great men in the non-military sphere: E. Badian in T. A. Dorey (ed.) *Latin Historians* (1966) 8; 30 note 36

4 *Origines* fr. 83 *HRR*. The passage gives a good example of the whole complex *virtus-virtutes-gloria* in action. Compare, *e.g.* Caedicius' words 'ego hanc tibi et rei publicae animam do' with Ennius, *Annales* fr. 200–2 *ROL* I, quoted above p. 24

5 *Origines* fr. 83 *HRR*: 'dii immortales tribuno militum fortunam ex virtute eius dedere . . . isque convaluit saepeque postilla operam rei publicae fortem atque strenuam perhibuit'

6 Nepos, *Cato* 3; Cato *Origines* fr. 73; 76 *HRR*

7 Cato, *Origines* fr. 51 *HRR*

8 Cato, *Origines* fr. 95; 106 *HRR*

9 Cato, *Origines* fr. 113–15; 118; 132 *HRR*. According to fr. 118 it had been

the *mos* of the *maiores* at banquets to sing 'clarorum virorum laudes atque virtutes'

10 Cato fr. 69; 58; 59 and the speech against Ser. Galba on behalf of the plundered Lusitanians, *ORF*[2]

11 Cato fr. 58; 97; *cf.* 94 *ORF*[2]

12 Cato fr. 224 *ORF*[2]

13 Cato fr. 112 *ORF*[2]. Contrast Ennius on the friend of Servilius, above pp. 24f

14 Cato fr. 94 *ORF*[2]

15 *Cf.* Cato fr. 94; 141 *ORF*[2]

16 Cicero, *De Senectute* 14. See, for instance, Cato's censorial speeches *De Vestitu et Vehiculis* and *De Signis et Tabulis*, his defence of the *lex Orchia* which limited the size and expensiveness of banquets, his support of the *lex Voconia* designed to prevent women gaining control of large amounts of capital and thus to check the growing emancipation of women. On these and other speeches by Cato see *ORF*[2] and H. H. Scullard, *Roman Politics*, Appendix II, 256ff

17 Cato fr. 185 (building); 98; 110 (furniture); 96; 145; 146 (cookery), *ORF*[2]

18 *Cf.* Cato fr. 64; 94; 141; 146 *ORF*[2]

19 *Cf.* Cato fr. 18; 144; 200, *ORF*[2]

20 *Cf.* Cato fr. 18; 144 *ORF*[2]; Plutarch, *Cato Maior* 1, 1. Cato's grandfather may even not have been a full Roman citizen, *cf.* H. H. Scullard, *Roman Politics*, 111

21 Cato fr. 203; *cf.* 173; 83; 122 *ORF*[2]

22 Cato fr. 51; 53; 54; *cf.* 132 *ORF*[2]

23 Cato fr. 128; 131 *HRR*; 66 *ORF*[2]

24 Cato fr. 174 *ORF*[2]; *cf.* Plutarch, *Cato Maior* 4, 4

25 Plutarch, *Cato Maior* 19, 5. For *virtus* (=ἀρετή) see Sallust's adaptation; 'non divitiis cum divite neque factione cum factioso sed cum strenuo virtute . . . certabat', *B.C.* 54, 6, *cf.* D. C. Earl, *The Political Thought of Sallust*, 100f

26 *Cf.* Cato fr. 93; 252 *ORF*[2]

27 Cato fr. 128 *ORF*[2]

28 Cicero, *Pro Sestio* 136; *cf.* Q. Cicero, *Comment. de Pet.* 7; Cicero, *Pro Murena* 17; *De Lege Agraria* II, 3; *In Verrem* II, iii, 7; v, 180. On what follows see D. C. Earl *The Political Thought of Sallust*, chapter III

29 Cicero, *In Verrem* II, v, 180

30 *Cf.* M. Gelzer, *Nobilität*, 28; J. Vogt, *Homo Novus* (1926), 24 note 4. The present discussion, like most modern treatments, is founded on Vogt's work

31 *Cf.* Cicero, *In Pisonem* 2f; *De Lege Agraria* II, 100; *In Verrem* II, iii, 7; iv, 81; v, 180ff

32 Cicero, *In Pisonem* 2; *cf.* H. Last in *CAH* IX 138f

33 Cicero, *Pro Sestio* 136; *Pro Balbo* 51; *Pro Murena* 17; *In Verrem* II, iv, 81
34 Cicero, *In Verrem* II, iv, 81
35 Sallust, *B.J.* 85, 4: 'vetus nobilitas, maiorum fortia facta, cognatorum et adfinium opes, multae clientelae'; 85, 37: 'nobilitas . . . omnis honores non ex merito sed quasi debitos a vobis repetit'; 85, 29: 'imagines . . . triumphos aut consulatus maiorum'; 85, 38: 'divitas, imagines, memoriam sui praeclaram'
36 Sallust, *B.J.* 85, 7; 29; 33; 5; 1; 9; *cf.* 63, 3
37 Sallust, *B.J.* 85, 30
38 Sallust, *B.J.* 85, 38
39 Sallust, *B.J.* 85, 15
40 Sallust, *B.J.* 85, 17
41 Sallust, *B.J.* 85, 38
42 Sallust, *B.J.* 85, 16; 17; 36
43 See A. N. Sherwin-White, *J.R.S.* 1956, 2ff; T. Carney, *A Biography of Marius*, 22ff; D. C. Earl, *The Political Thought of Sallust*, 71ff; 76ff; *Latomus*, 1965, 532ff
44 Sallust, *B.J.* 86, 3
45 Cicero, *In Verrem* II, v, 81; *Pro Plancio* 12; *Pro Rab. Perd.* 21; *De Officiis* III, 77; for Fimbria see Valerius Maximus VIII, 2, 4; for Billienus, Cicero, *Brutus* 175
46 *Cf.* D. C. Earl, *The Political Thought of Sallust*, 77; *J.R.S.* 1965, 235f; *Historia*, 1966, 302ff
47 Sallust, *B.J.* 63, 6; *B.C.* 23, 6
48 Sallust, *B.C.* 31, 7; Cicero *Pro Sulla* 22
49 Cicero, *Pro Sext. Rosc. Am.* 16; 136
50 D. C. Earl, *The Political Thought of Sallust*, 37
51 *Cf.* A. N. Sherwin-White, *J.R.S.* 1956, 2ff; E. Badian, *Foreign Clientelae*, 203f
52 E. Badian, *Studies in Greek and Roman History*, 56; 215
53 The opportunities for advancement under Sulla became proverbial, *cf. e.g.* Sallust, *B.C.* 37, 6. Similarly in the sixties of the first century BC connection with Pompey was profitable both to new men and to personal adherents, like A. Plautius, M. Terentius Varro, L. Afranius, M. Petreius and A. Gabinius, and even to *nobiles* seeking profit and advancement in their careers: R. Syme, *Roman Revolution*, 32. Similarly with Caesar in the fifties, although the complicated political situation reduced the effectiveness of Caesar's patronage
54 *Cf.* what Cicero said about Pompey's father: 'hominem dis ac nobilitati perinvisum', Asconius p. 79, Clark
55 *Cf.* A. N. Sherwin-White, *J.R.S.* 1956
56 See further D. C. Earl, *The Political Thought of Sallust*, 28ff
57 *Cf. e.g. CIL* I^2 10: 'honos fama virtusque gloria atque ingenium'
58 Sallust, *B.C.* 3; *B.J.* 4, *Cf.* above pp. 23ff

59 See the works cited above p. 136 note 49

60 On these terms see H. Strasburger, *P-W s.v.* 'Optimates', XVII, 773ff; R. Syme, *Roman Revolution*, 11; 16; 65; 72; 153. Ch. Meier, *P-W s.v.* 'Populares', Supplb. X, 549ff

61 R. Syme, *Roman Revolution*, 154ff; C. Wirszubski, *Libertas as a Political Idea at Rome* (1950), chapters II and III; D. C. Earl, *The Political Thought of Sallust*, 54ff; 106ff

62 *Bell. Afr.* 22, 2; Caesar, *B.C.* 22, 5

63 Sallust, *B.C.* 38, 3–4

64 And, of course, to the period covered by the *Histories*, the remains of which are too fragmentary to permit detailed analysis

65 His shortcomings in both departments will be found discussed in D. C. Earl, *The Political Thought of Sallust* and *J.R.S.* 1965, 235ff; R. Syme, *Sallust* (1964)

66 On the Spanish Wars see, in addition to the standard histories, H. Simon, *Roms Krieg im Spanien, 154–133 v. Chr.* (1962), and, briefly, D. C. Earl, *Tiberius Gracchus*, 109ff

67 *Cf.* E. Badian, *Foreign Clientelae*, 272; 281; *Studies*, 225

68 Sallust, *B.C.* 35; *cf.* D. C. Earl, *The Political Thought of Sallust*, 94f; R. Syme, *Sallust*, 71f

69 Florus II, 13, 11; Dio Cassius XXXVII, 55, 3–56, 4

70 Florus II, 13, 14

71 Florus II, 13, 14; Lucan I, 125; Caesar, *B.C.* I, 4, 4; Velleius Paterculus II, 33, 3

72 Caesar, *B.C.* I, 9, 2: 'sibi semper primam fuisse dignitatem vitaque potiorem'; *cf.* 7, 7; III, 91, 2; Cicero, *Pro Ligario* 18; *Pro Marcello* 25; Hirtius *B.G.* VIII, 52, 4; 53, 1

73 Cicero, *Ad Att.* VII, 11, 1: 'utrum de imperatore populi Romani an de Hannibale loquimur? . . . atque haec ait omnia facere se dignitatis causa'. Suetonius, *Divus Iulius* 72, records a saying of Caesar: 'If he had used the help of bandits and thugs in defending his *dignitas*, he would have given even them an appropriate reward.' Caesar's political alliance with men of the lowest sort was notorious to contemporaries, *cf. e.g.* Cicero, *Ad Fam.* VIII, 4, 2

CHAPTER III

1 Horace, *Odes* II, 7, 11

2 Cicero, *Ad Att.* VIII, 11, 2

3 Livy XXXVIII, 54, 1 and 6; *cf.* 51, 3–4; Polybius X, 40; H. H. Scullard, *Roman Politics*, 83; 85

4 Cicero, *De Amicitia* 40. On Ti. Gracchus' *regnum* see D. C. Earl, *Tiberius Gracchus*, 105ff

5 C. Wirszubski, *Libertas*, 62

6 Sallust, *B.C.* 5, 6

7 Cicero, *De Lege Agraria* I, 24; *Ad Att.* I, 16, 10; *Pro Sulla* 21; 25; *cf. Pro Sestio* 109; *De Domo* 85; 94

8 C. Wirszubski, *Libertas*, 14; *cf.* D. C. Earl, *The Political Thought of Sallust*, 106f; W. Allen, *T.A.P.A.* 1953, 227

9 *Bell. Afr.* 22, 2; 'paene oppressam funditus et deletam Italiam urbemque Romam in libertatem vindicavit', from a speech attributed to the younger Cato

10 Caesar, *B.C.* I, 22, 5: 'ut se et populum Romanum factione paucorum oppressum in libertatem vindicaret'

11 R. Syme, *Roman Revolution*, 155

12 On the *clementia Caesaris* see M. Treu, *Museum Helveticum* 1948, 197ff; for the hostility of Caesar's *regnum* to *virtus cf.* Cicero *Orator* 35: 'tempora timens inimica virtuti'

13 Cicero, *Pro Marcello* 2; 18; 22; *Pro Ligario* 15

14 Cicero, *Pro Ligario* 13

15 *Cf.* Seneca, *De Clementia* I, 3, 3; 20, 3; II, 3, 1. On Caesar's *clementia* and its implications see also Plutarch, *Cato Minor* 66

16 On Brutus' *De Virtute* see H. Bardon, *La Litterature latin inconnue* (1952), 210f

17 *Cf.* R. Syme, *Roman Revolution*, 57

18 Brutus fr. 16 *ORF*²: 'praestat enim nemini imperare quam alicui servire: sine illo enim vivere honeste licet, cum hoc vivendi nulla condicio est', *cf.* fr. 17

19 Lucan IX, 204f; *cf.* Tacitus, *Hist.* II, 38

20 See R. Syme, *Roman Revolution*, 238f; 291, 328; 368; 372f; 376ff; 382; 404f; 419ff; 453; 490ff; 510f

21 *Cf.* Cicero's alleged remark: 'laudandum adulescentem, ornandum, tollendum', *Ad Fam.* XI, 20, 1; *cf.* R. Syme, *Roman Revolution*, 181f

22 On Octavian's early support see R. Syme, *Roman Revolution*, 128ff

23 R. Syme, *Roman Revolution*, 133

24 R. Syme, *Roman Revolution*, 228f; 238f

25 *Cf.* A. H. M. Jones, *Studies*, 12; it may be that in 19 BC Augustus received *imperium consulare*, *cf. id. Studies*, 13ff

26 I speak now of these ideas as they were actually applied to practical politics, not of special and quasi-philosophical definitions and treatments, such as Cicero's *De Republica*, which stand apart from and had no influence on the realities of political life. For a convenient collection of material and bibliography on the development of the notion of *respublica* in literature, see W. Suerbaum, *Vom antiken zum frühmittelalterlichen Staatsbegriff*, 1961

27 *Cf.* C. Wirszubski, *Libertas*, 121

28 *Res Gestae Divi Augusti* 1

29 Velleius Paterculus II, 89, 4: 'prisca illa et antiqua rei publicae forma revocata'; Suetonius, *Divus Augustus* 28, 2

30 Virgil, *Aeneid* I, 566; II, 367; V, 258; 455; 754; VI, 806; VIII, 548; IX, 741; 795; X, 410; 712; 752; 872; XI, 27; 312; 386; 415; XII, 668; 714; 913

31 Virgil, *Aeneid* II, 390; XII, 435f; 714

32 Virgil, *Aeneid* X, 467ff; 'stat sua cuique dies, breve et inreparabile tempus/omnibus est vitae: sed famam extendere factis/hoc virtutis opus'

33 *Cf.* Virgil, *Aeneid* V, 342ff; 363ff; X, 367ff; XII, 435ff. *Honos* (and *honores*) as *praemia virtutis* was by Virgil's time a traditional formulation

34 *Cf.* Virgil, *Aeneid* III, 341ff; X, 367ff; XII, 435ff

35 *Cf.* Virgil, *Aeneid* VI, 129ff; IX, 641ff

36 See above pp. 30f

37 Virgil *Aeneid* XI, 440ff

38 On Turnus see V. Pöschl, *The Art of Virgil* (1962), 91ff. and the discussions to which he refers

39 Virgil, *Aeneid* VII, 55f; 473f; 650

40 Virgil, *Aeneid* VII, 469: 'tutari Italiam, detrudere finibus hostem'; IX, 22ff; V. Pöschl, *The Art of Virgil*, 97

41 Virgil, *Aeneid* XII, 19f

42 *Cf.* Pöschl, *The Art of Virgil*, 98f

43 Virgil, *Aeneid* I, 639–97; II, 504; III, 475; V, 268; 473; VII, 12; VIII, 202; 683; 721; XII, 126

44 *Cf.* Virgil, *Aeneid* VIII, 481ff; XI, 14ff; II, 785ff; III, 325ff; VIII, 196f; 612ff; XI, 539f; XII, 236f. Between the two extremes there is room for subjective interpretation. Thus Troy is described as *superbum/regnatorem Asiae*, II, 556f; *cf.* III, 1ff; to Iuno the Romans are *superbi*, I, 21f, as are Aeneas and his ships to Dido, IV, 424; 540f, and the commands of Iuppiter to Iuturna, XII, 876ff. At VI, 817 I take *animamque superbam* with *Tarquinios reges*, as Leo and Norden

45 Virgil, *Aeneid* X, 445ff; *cf.* IX, 634f; X, 514; XII, 326f

46 Virgil, *Aeneid* I, 522; VI, 851ff

47 Virgil, *Aeneid* I, 33: 'tantae molis erat Romanam condere gentem'

48 *Cf.* Iuno's words, XII, 826: 'sit Latium, sint Albani per saecula reges/sit Romana potens Itala virtute propago', and the scene on the shield of Aeneas, VIII, 678f: 'hinc Augustus agens Italos in proelia Caesar/cum patribus populoque, penatibus et magnis dis'

49 Virgil, *Aeneid* XI, 336ff. In the only two occurrences of the adjective *nobilis* Virgil reverted to its root-meaning, 'well-known', and used it not of people but of places, *Aeneid* VII, 564; VIII, 341

50 *Cf.* Virgil, *Aeneid* V, 394ff; IX, 278ff; XI, 154ff

51 *Cf.* Virgil, *Aeneid* IV, 229ff; 272ff; *cf.* 47ff; VI, 756ff

52 *Cf.* Pöschl, *The Art of Virgil*, 40ff

53 Virgil, *Aeneid* I, 544f

54 *Cf.* Virgil, *Aeneid* I, 603f; VI, 620f
55 *Cf.* Virgil, *Aeneid* I, 523
56 Virgil, *Aeneid* VIII, 670
57 Sallust, *B.C.* 54
58 Virgil, *Aeneid* VIII, 678ff
59 Horace, *Odes* III, 26, 2; *Sat.* I, 6, 23f; II, 3, 179ff
60 Horace, *Odes* III, 26, 2
61 Horace, *Odes* I, 18, 14ff
62 Horace, *Sat.* I, 6, 23f; *cf. Epist.* II, 1, 177f
63 Horace, *Epist.* I, 18, 21f
64 Horace, *Sat.* II, 3, 179ff
65 Horace, *Odes* III, 2, 13
66 Horace, *Odes* I, 8, 12; 12, 25ff; 29, 13ff; III, ii, 33ff; 13, 13ff; IV, 3, 12; *Epod.* 9, 29; 13, 11; *Epist.* II 3, 137; 258f
67 *Cf. Odes* I, 1, 5–6; 14, 11ff
68 Horace, *Odes* IV, 12, 15; 1, 13; III, 17, 1ff
69 Horace, *Epist.* I, 19, 37ff. On this passage *cf.* E. Fraenkel, *Horace* (1957) 348f
70 *Cf.* Horace, *Odes* I, 14, 11ff
71 Horace, *Epist.* I, 18, 9; *cf.* II, 6, 16; *Sat.* II, 6, 72ff; Aristotle, *Eth. Nic.* II, 6; Horace, *Sat.* I, 10, 5f; E. Fraenkel, *Horace*, 128
72 Horace, *Epist.* I, 17, 41f; *cf. ibid.* 38; *Epod.* 15, 11f; *Epist.* I, 6, 29ff; I, 1, 41ff; II, 2, 37f
73 Horace, *Epist.* I, 2, 17ff
74 Horace, *Sat.* II, 3, 9ff; 94ff; *cf. Epod.* 16, 39f; *Sat.* I, 9, 54ff; *Epist.* II, 3, 289ff; 370f
75 *Cf.* Horace, *Sat.* I, 3, 38–75; 6, 82ff; II, 2, 1ff; *Epist.* I, 12, 7ff; 16, 52; 65ff; 11, 3, 42ff
76 Horace, *Odes*, III, 24; 6, 33ff; *Epod.* 2; *cf.* E. Fraenkel, *Horace*, 241
77 In addition to the passages cited above, *e.g. Epist.* II, 1, 118ff on the *virtutes* of poetry and I, 18, 21ff on the *virtutes* of the client. See also *Odes* IV, 14 1ff on Augustus
78 Horace *Odes* IV, 5, 29f; III, 5, 26ff; *Epod.* 9, 25ff; *Sat.* II, 1, 72; *Odes* III, 21, 11ff; *Sat.* I, 2, 31f; *Epist.* I, 19, 12f
79 Horace, *Epist.* I, 1, 16ff. This notion of *vera virtus* may be Stoic as all the commentators insist; it is certainly the traditional Roman attitude as far back as we can trace it. For the main divisions of public life *cf. Epist.* II, 1, 230: 'belli spectata domique/virtus'
80 Horace, *Odes* III, 2, 17ff
81 *Odes* IV, 14, 1ff; *Epist.* II, 1, 1ff
82 Horace, *Epist.* II, 1, 48ff
83 Horace, *Epist.* I, 20, 20ff
84 *Cf.* above chapter II

85 Horace, *Odes* IV, 4, 29ff; *cf. Epist.* I, 12, 26f

86 T. Mommsen, *Staatsrecht*, I^3, 94; 135f; II^3, 260; 848. Horace fully understood the position in this Ode and its companion for Drusus' brother Tiberius, IV, 14: see E. Fraenkel, *Horace*, 431f. *Cf.* the case of M. Licinius Crassus who claimed the *spolia opima*, R. Syme, *Roman Revolution*, 308f; *cf.* 404

87 *Cf.* Horace, *Odes* IV, 4, 34ff

88 Horace, *Carm. Saec.* 53ff. *Cf. Sat.* I, 7, 14 on the disruptive potentiality of *virtus*

89 Virgil, *Aeneid* XII, 190f; *cf.* I, 263f

90 Horace, *Odes* III, 14, 14ff

91 Horace, *Odes* IV, 15, 17ff

92 Plutarch, *Brutus*, 12

93 The unity Rome–Italy is as prominent in Horace as in Virgil. *cf. e.g.* Horace, *Odes* II, 7, 3f; 13, 18; III, 5, 40; IV, 14, 7; 14, 44; 15, 13; *Carm. Saec.* 66; *Sat.* I, 6, 35; *Epist.* I, 12, 25ff; 18, 57; II, 1, 2. Horace also agreed with Virgil as to the position of Cato, *cf. Odes* I, 12, 35f; II, 1 21ff; *cf.* Augustus' own view, Macrobius II, 4, 18

94 Livy I, 9, 3

95 Livy II, 12, especially 9: 'Romanus sum, inquit, civis. C. Mucium vocant. hostis hostem occidere volui nec ad mortem minus animi est quam fuit ad caedem; et facere et pati fortia Romanum est'; 13: 'en tibi, inquit, ut sentias quam vile corpus sit iis qui magnam gloriam vident'; 14: 'tu vero abi, inquit (Porsenna), in te magnis quam in me hostilia ausus. iuberem macte virtute esse, si pro mea patria ista virtus staret.' For *honos* due to *virtus* see 12, 15; 13, 5; *cf.* III, 63, 9: 'pro virtute honorem pati'. *Cf.* H. Hoch, *Die Darstellung der politische Sendung Roms* (1951) Chap. II

96 Livy II, 13, 9

97 Livy III, 12, 2ff; *cf.* 19, 5

98 Livy IV, 14, 7

99 Livy XXVIII, 17, 2f

100 *E.g.* Livy I, 32, 2; 35, 1; II, 15, 7; 22, 5; 40, 11f; III, 21, 7; 24, 11; 44, 3; 58, 4; 68, 5; IV, 10, 7; 11, 1; 12, 8

101 Livy I, 53, 4

102 Livy V, 27, 6f; XLII, 47. On the latter passage see F. W. Walbank, *J.R.S.* 1965, 3ff

103 Livy V, 27, 11ff

104 Livy XXII, 3, 4f; *cf.* XXI, 63, 13. For further examples of these moral standards and Livy's attitude see P. Walsh, *Livy* (1961), 66–109, though with reservations on Stoic influence

105 Livy XXI, 4, 3ff; *cf.* Sallust, *B.C.* 5

106 Livy *praef.* 11ff. *Cf.* R. M. Ogilvie, *A Commentary on Livy Books 1–5* (1965), 23ff; R. Syme, *Harvard Studies in Classical Philology*, 1959, 42f

107 *Cf.* Livy II, 10, 6: 'Sp. Larcium ac T. Herminium ambos claros genere factisque'
108 *Cf.* Livy III, 11, 6
109 Livy IV, 3, 13–17; *cf.* IV, 5, 5: 'si aditus ad honores viris strenuis et fortibus datur', and above, chapter II, on the *novi homines*
110 Livy I, 34, 6
111 For what little is known of Livy's life see P. Walsh, *Livy*, 1ff; R. M. Ogilvie, *Livy Books 1–5*, 1ff
112 Suetonius, *Claudius* 41, 1
113 Livy I, 19, 3; XXVIII, 12, 12; *Periocha* LIX
114 *Cf.* R. Syme, *Harvard Studies*, 1959, 43ff; R. M. Ogilvie, *Livy Books 1–5*, 563f
115 I do not, of course, intend to imply that Livy consciously wrote against the reinterpretation of the ideal found in Virgil and Horace. On the use of *princeps* by Livy see R. M. Ogilvie, *Livy Books 1–5*, 392
116 Tacitus, *Ann.* IV, 34, 3

CHAPTER IV

1 Tacitus, *Agricola*, 42, 5
2 There can have been few like Q. Haterius, *cos. suff.* 5 BC. Born in or about the consulship of Cicero, he died in AD 26, aged nearly ninety. He claimed to be one of the few who had 'seen the Republic' and was apt to declaim about Cicero and liberty, *cf.* Tacitus, *Ann.* I, 13, 6; Seneca, *Suas.* IV, 1f; VII, 1
3 Tacitus, *Hist.* IV, 17
4 Tacitus, *Ger.* 20, 2
5 *Cf. e.g.* Tacitus, *Ger.* 30, 2; *Hist.* III, 60; I, 15; *Ann.* I, 21; IV, 39; VI, 22; XV, 5; 48
6 *Cf.* Tacitus, *Hist.* IV, 29
7 *Cf.* Tacitus, *Hist.* II, 82; *Ann.* XVI, 6
8 *Cf.* Tacitus, *Hist.* II, 69; IV, 73; *Agr.* 33, 2
9 *Cf.* Tacitus, *Ann.* XV, 16
10 *Cf.* Tacitus, *Ann.* XIII, 54. For further passages connecting *virtus*, *gloria*, etc., *cf. e.g. Hist.* II, 57; III, 9; V, 17; *Ann.* II, 60; XIV, 15; *Ger.* 42, 1
11 Tacitus, *Hist.* III, 51
12 Tacitus, *Agr.* 41, 4; *cf.* 8, 2; *Ann.* IV, 40
13 Tacitus, *Ann.* IV, 38
14 Tacitus, *Ann.* II, 73; III, 5
15 *Cf.* Tacitus, *Agr.* 1; 46, 1
16 Tacitus, *Ann.* XI, 22
17 Tacitus, *Hist.* I, 72; *cf.* II, 82
18 *Cf.* Tacitus, *Hist.* I, 91; I, 30

19 *Cf.* Tacitus, *Agr.* 44, 3

20 For *bonae artes/virtutes cf. e.g. Ann.* XI, 22 and *Hist.* I, 72; also *Ann.* II, 73; III, 70; *Hist.* I, 10; 30; *Ann.* I, 9

21 See *e.g. Agr.* 9, 4; *Hist.* II, 5; I, 10; II, 77; *Agr.* 11, 5; *Hist.* II, 62; *Ann.* XV 2; *Hist.* III, 11; IV, 2; *Agr.* 32, 1; *Ann.* I, 75; *Hist.* III, 38; *Ann.* III, 47; 62; I, 15; 58; XV, 20

22 Tacitus, *Hist.* I, 3

23 Tacitus, *Hist.* II, 5

24 *Cf. e.g. Hist.* I, 52; 71; III, 77; *Ann.* IV, 71; VI, 51

25 *Cf. Hist.* III, 77

26 Tacitus, *Ann.* XV, 48

27 Tacitus, *Hist.* I, 49

28 Tacitus, *Ger.* 7, 1

29 *Cf. Ann.* XI, 17

30 For the decline of the *nobiles* see R. Syme, *Roman Revolution*, 490ff

31 *Cf.* Velleius Paterculus II, 71 2f

32 The notorious informer, Porcius Cato, *cos. suff.* AD 36, Tacitus, *Ann.* IV, 68ff, may not have belonged to the family of Cato Uticensis

33 Tacitus, *Ann.* I, 2

34 *Cf.* Tacitus, *Hist.* I, 49

35 *Cf.* Suetonius, *Divus Vespasianus*, 1

36 Juvenal, *Sat.* VIII

37 *Cf.* Tacitus, *Ann.* XIII, 18: '(Agrippina) nomina et virtutes nobilium, qui etiam superant, in honore habere, quasi quaereret ducem et partes'

38 Suetonius, *Divus Iulius*, 80, 2. On Caesar's new senators see R. Syme, *Roman Revolution*, 78ff; *P.B.S.R.* 1938, 1ff. On the rise of the provincials see R. Syme, *Tacitus*, 585ff

39 Dio Cassius LIX, 9, 5. P Memmius Regulus, *cos. suff.* AD 31 was probably of Narbonese origin, E. Badian, *Foreign Clientelae*, 317ff. R. Syme, *Tacitus*, 787

40 Tacitus, *Ann.* XI, 23f; *ILS* 212; *cf.* R. Syme, *Tacitus*, 317ff and Appendix 40

41 See R. Syme, *Tacitus*, 597

42 *Cf.* P. Lambrechts, *La Composition du sénat romain de l'accession au trône d'Hadrien à la mort de Commode* (1936); R. Syme, *Roman Revolution*, 505

43 Tacitus, *Ann.* III, 55; *cf.* 52

44 *Cf.* Tacitus *Ann.* XII, 53

45 Tacitus, *Ann.* XVI, 5

46 *Cf.* Seneca's words in Tacitus, *Ann.* XIV, 53 and the description of Massilia in *Agr.* 4, 3

47 *Cf. e.g. Agr.* 1, 4; *Ann.* III, 65; *Hist.* I, 3

48 Tacitus, *Ann.* I, 80

49 Tacitus, *Hist.* I, 2

50 Tacitus, *Agr.* 41, 1; *cf.* 4, 1

51 Tacitus, *Agr.* 39, 3
52 Tacitus, *Ann.* IV, 33; *Agr.* 31, 4
53 *Cf.* Galba's words *Hist.* I, 16
54 *Cf. Hist.* IV, 5
55 Tacitus, *Agr.* 42, 5; *c. Ann.* XIV, 12 on Thrasea Paetus: 'sibi causam periculi fecit, ceteris libertatis initium non praebuit'. Later Thrasea dissuaded the young Arulenus Rusticus from uselessly incurring danger, *Ann.* XVI, 26
56 *Cf. Ger.* 6–27 passim; Seneca, *De Ira* I, 11, 4
57 Tacitus, *Ger.* 14, 1
58 Tacitus, *Ann.* VI, 8
59 *Cf. e.g. Hist.* I, 21
60 Tacitus, *Agr.* 4, 1. Both his grandfathers had been procurators under, probably, Augustus and Tiberius
61 *Agr.* 4, 4
62 *Cf. e.g. Hist.* IV, 5: Helvidius studied philosophy 'non ut plerique, ut nomine magnifico segne otium velaret, sed quo firmior adversus fortuita rem publicam capesseret'
63 *Agr.* 4, 5
64 *Agr.* 5
65 *Agr.* 6
66 *Agr.* 7
67 *Agr.* 8; *cf. Ger.* 14, 2
68 *Agr.* 9
69 *Agr.* 38–42. We are here concerned merely with Tacitus' presentation, but it must be mentioned that this presentation is open to question as a statement of historical fact; see *e.g.* T. A. Dorey, *Greece and Rome*, 1960, 66ff; H. W. Traub, *C.Ph.* 1954, 255ff; K. von Fritz, *C.Ph.* 1957, 73ff
70 *Cf. Hist.* I, 1: 'dignitatem nostram a Vespasiano inchoatam, a Tito auctam, a Domitiano longius provectam non abnuerim'
71 R. Syme, *Tacitus*, 26
72 Tacitus, *Ann.* I, 2; *cf. Hist.* I, 19; 85; II, 90f; III, 37
73 Tacitus, *Ann.* III, 65
74 Tacitus, *Ann.* IV, 20. On Marcus (not Manius) Lepidus, see R. Syme, *J.R.S.* 1955, 22ff
75 Tacitus, *Ann.* XIV, 47
76 Tacitus, *Hist.* IV, 8
77 Pliny, *Pan.* 9, 3; *cf.* 5: 'obsequii gloria'
78 *Ann.* III, 55. *Cf.* the speech of Valerius Messalinus, *Ann.* III, 34; *Hist.* I, 3

CHAPTER V

1 Ammianus Marcellinus XIV, 6, 3. Throughout this chapter I am deeply indebted to Edward Gibbon, *The Decline and Fall of the Roman Empire* and A. H. M. Jones, *The Later Roman Empire 284–602* (1964). Fully to acknow-

ledge my obligations to these two works would require annotation of almost every sentence. I trust that I shall not be accounted niggardly if I ask instead to be allowed to make this general acknowledgement.

Ammianus Marcellinus is quoted from the edition of C. U. Clark, Berlin (1910–15, reprinted 1963). The translations, as elsewhere, are my own, but the peculiarities of Ammianus' text and style have frequently driven me to paraphrase in order to render what I take to be his meaning in something approaching acceptable English.

2 *Cf. e.g.* Cicero; Tacitus, *Ann.* XV, 44

3 R. Syme, *Tacitus*, 530; Juvenal *Sat.* III, 61

4 On Trajan and his family see R. Syme, *Tacitus*, 30ff

5 Ammianus XXVIII, 1, 23. In XXIX, 2, 17 the whole *ordo* murmurs against a decision of Valens

6 A. H. M. Jones, *Later Roman Empire*, 331

7 Pliny *Ep.* VI, 19, 4

8 Ammianus XXVI, 7, 10; *cf.* 16

9 On Ammianus see, especially, W. Ennslin, *Klio*, Beiheft xvi, 1923; E. A. Thompson, *The Historical Work of Ammianus Marcellinus* (1947); Henry T. Rowell, *Ammianus Marcellinus, Soldier-Historian of the Late Roman Empire* (1964)

10 Henry T. Rowell, *Ammianus Marcellinus*, 30

11 Ammianus XIV, 2, 8

12 Ammianus XIV, 2, 1ff; XIX, 13, 1; XXVII, 9, 6

13 Ammianus XXXVIII, 2, 11ff

14 Ammianus XIV, 7, 5; *cf.* the riots at Antioch, XXXI, 1, 2

15 Ammianus XX, 1, 1; XXVII, 8

16 Ammianus XV, 5, 2; 8, 1; XXVIII, 2, 10

17 Ammianus XVI, 10, 20

18 Ammianus XXVII, 9, 1ff; XXVIII, 6, 2ff

19 Ammianus XXVI, 4, 5f; *cf.* 5, 6f. For Persian depredations under Constantius see *e.g.* XV, 13, 4; XVI, 9, 1ff

20 For a recent discussion of Ammianus' Roman *exempla* see J. Vogt, *Ammianus Marcellinus als Erzählender Geschichtsschreiber der Spätzeit* (1963). To list these *exempla* would be tedious, but to give the reader some idea of the extent of Ammianus' practice it may be mentioned that in the eighteen extant books of his *History* there are close on one hundred such references to Roman history in addition to over thirty quotations from Cicero. Greek references are far fewer and are as often literary as historical

21 Ammianus XIV, 6, 2

22 See *e.g.* Ammianus XIV, 6, 7–24; 25; XV, 7, 3; XIX, 10; XXVI, 14f; XXVII, 3; XXVIII, 4, 6–27; 28–35

23 Ammianus XIV, 6, 4ff

24 Ammianus XIV, 6, 3

25 Livy I, 9, 3

26 *Cf. e.g.* Ammianus XIX, 10, 4; XXVI, 1, 14; XXVII, 6, 6. Ammianus observed the double attitude to *fortuna*, though it is scarcely remarkable if in the times in which he lived he was more impressed by Fortune as capricious and malignant chance. On the one hand the fickle changes of Fortune 'mock at mortal men, now lifting some to the stars, now drowning them in the depths of Cocytus', XIV, 11, 29; *cf. e.g.* XXI, 16, 13–14; XXXI, 1, 1; 8, 8. On the other hand, Fortune assists good designs, XXVI, 2, 9; XV, 8, 2. On Julian's *felicitas* see below p. 116

27 Ammianus XXIX, 2, 16

28 Ammianus XX, 4, 1; *cf.* XV, 2, 1

29 Ammianus XVI, 10, 3; *cf.* XIV, 6, 21

30 *Cf.* Ammianus XV, 4, 3

31 Ammianus XVI, 12, 3; XVII, 5, 6. Sapor is described as writing 'in no way swerving from his inborn arrogance', XVII, 5, 1, and just before the sentence quoted in the text is made to recognize the possibility that his description of himself as 'surpassing the kings of old in splendour and in multitude of outstanding *virtutes*' might, by Roman standards, appear arrogant

32 Ammianus XIV, 6, 5

33 Ammianus XXV, 5, 1ff

34 Ammianus XXVI, 1, 3ff; 2, 1ff

35 Ammianus XXX, 10, 1ff

36 Ammianus XXVI, 4, 1–3

37 Ammianus XX, 8, 12

38 Ammianus XV, 5, 25; 5, 22

39 Ammianus XXVI, 6, 12; 16. With 'dehonestamentum omnium honorum' compare Sallust *Hist.* I, 55, 22M. It is curious that the revolts both of Silvanus and of Procopius provoked Sallustian reminiscence in Ammianus. With Silvanus' expressed reason for revolt ('aegre ferebat Silvanus ad consulatum potestatesque sublimes elatis indignis se et Ursicinum solos post exsudatos magnos pro re publica labores et crebros ita fuisse despectos') compare Catiline in Sallust, *B.C.* 35, 3–5

40 Ammianus XXVI, 7, 12; 8, 1; 9, 5; XXXVII, 5, 1

41 Ammianus XXVI, 9, 10

42 Ammianus XIV, 7, 9ff

43 Ammianus XIV, 11, 24

44 Ammianus XXIII, 5, 17. Note the reaction of the Senate to a letter from Julian attacking Constantius. The nobles with one voice shouted 'auctori tuo reverentiam rogamus'—and Ammianus approved, *cf.* 8

45 Ammianus XXIX, 6, 7–8; *cf.* XVI, 4, 3; 7, 1

46 Ammianus XXI, 16, 1. *Cf.* the description of Constantius' entry into Rome, XVI, 10, 9ff

47 Ammianus XXII, 7, 1ff
48 Ammianus XXV, 4, 18
49 See, especially, Ammianus XXVI, 6, 15–16; 19
50 Ammianus XIX, 12, 17
51 Ammianus XIV, 7, 5; 10, 12; XV, 8, 21; XXIX, 2, 18; XXX, 8, 14. He should be 'parens publicus', XXIX, 2, 7
52 Ammianus XXX, 8, 2; *cf.* 10
53 *Cf.* Ammianus XIX, 12, 18
54 Ammianus XIV, 1, 4; XV, 1, 3
55 Ammianus XXIX, 2, 18
56 Ammianus XV, 10, 7
57 Ammianus XVI, 5, 12; XXVI, 10, 10. For an example of injustice under Julian which also demonstrates Ammianus' concept of a subject's loyalty to his emperor, *cf.* XXII, 3, 4
58 Ammianus XXIX, 1, 18ff
59 Ammianus XXIX, 1, 27; 37; 2, 3
60 Ammianus XXX, 4, 1ff
61 Ammianus XIX, 12, 17
62 Ammianus XXIX, 5, 43
63 *Cf.* Ammianus XXIII, 1, 7. The emperor's duty was to fight, not buy off the barbarians, which was ultimately detrimental to the state and ineffective, XXIV, 3, 4; XXV, 6, 10
64 Ammianus XXVII, 7; XXIX, 3; XXVII, 9, 4
65 Ammianus XXIX, 4, 1. But Ammianus judged Valentinian excessive even in this laudable object, XXIX, 6, 2
66 Ammianus XXIX, 2, 14; XXX, 2, 3
67 Ammianus XXVII, 6, 12
68 *Cf.* above p. 24
69 Ammianus XV, 8, 12f. The contrast between Constantius' words and the actions of that most suspicious of emperors is striking
70 Ammianus XXI, 5, 3ff
71 Justice, *e.g.* XVIII, 1, 1f; XXII, 10; *cf.* XVII, 3; XVIII, 1. Self-control and moral standards, *e.g.* XXII, 4, 1–5; 9–10; XXV, 2, 2; 3, 18. Military ability, XIV–XXV, passim. See also the summary of his *virtutes*, XVI, 5, and the necrology, XXV, 4. Note, too, his proper sense of subordination as Caesar, XVI, 12, 27; XX, 4, 4; XVI, 12, 64
72 *E.g.* XVI, 3; 5; 11, 7; XVII, 9, 1; XX, 4, 8; XXII, 7, 7ff; XXIII, 5, 18ff
73 Ammianus XVIII, 2, 5
74 Ammianus XXII, 9, 1. *Concordia* was traditionally dependent on the *virtus* and *virtutes* of the citizen body and the re-establishment of *concordia* in a divided state the traditional attribute of the appointment to supreme power of a man of *virtus*
75 Ammianus XXIII, 5, 19. The Latin word rendered as 'given' is 'vovisse',

the technical term for the formal and solemn pledging oneself to death for the sake of the *respublica*

76 Ammianus XXV, 10, 5; *n.b.* 'ad perpetuandam gloriam recte factorum', *cf.* XXII, 9, 9ff

77 Ammianus XVI, 1, 2; *cf. e.g.* XVII, 1, 14; XXII, 2, 5; XXIV, 6, 4; XXV, 4, 14

78 Ammianus XV, 5

79 *Cf.* Ammianus XXI, 1, 2; XXII, 3, 3; 5; 11; 9, 16

80 Ammianus XXVI, 6, 7–9; 17; 8, 14

81 Ammianus XXVIII, 6; XXIX, 5

82 Ammianus XIX, 11, 7

83 Ammianus XXXI, 4, 4–5

84 Ammianus XXXI, 4, 9ff

85 Ammianus XXXI, 5, 4ff

86 Ammianus XXXI, 12, 7

87 Ammianus XXXI, 5, 14; *cf.* XV, 11, 4 on the Belgae

88 Ammianus XIV, 6, 25; XXVIII, 4, 28ff

89 Ammianus XIV, 6, 7ff; XXVIII, 4, 6ff

90 Ammianus XIV, 6, 7

91 Ammianus XXVIII, 4, 6

92 *E.g.* XIV, 6, 12, 18, 19, 24 'haec nobilium sunt instituta'

93 Ammianus XIV, 6, 10. *Cf.* the references to Acilius Glabrio and Cato the Censor in 8; to Valerius Publicola and the daughter of Cn. Cornelius Scipio in 11

94 Ammianus XVI, 10, 13

CHAPTER VI

1 Augustine, *De Civitate Dei* V, 18

2 We know the dates of neither Ammianus' birth nor his death. The closest we can get to the former is *c.* 325–30; for the latter all we know is that he did not die until after late 392 when Libanius (*Ep.* 1063) wrote to him in congratulation on the success of his *History*. For Ammianus' life see E. A. Thompson, *The Historical Work of Ammianus Marcellinus*

3 *Comm. in Ezek., praef.* The belief survived Alaric's sack. Bede, in the eighth century wrote: 'As long as the Coliseum stands, Rome shall stand; when the Coliseum falls, Rome will fall; when Rome falls, the world will fall', quoted by Edward Gibbon, *Decline and Fall*, chapter 71

4 Ammianus XXXI, 5, 1ff

5 *E.g. Civ. Dei* I, 35; X, 32; XI, 1; XV, 22; XVIII, 54; XIX, 17; 26

6 *Cf. Civ. Dei* XV, 1

7 *Civ. Dei* I, 15: 'cum aliud civitas non sit quam concors hominum multitudo'. On Augustine's use of *civitas, populus, respublica* see R. T. Marshall, *Studies in the Political and Socio-Religious Terminology of the De Civitate Dei* (1952)

8 Sallust, *B.C.* 6, 2; Augustine, *Epist.* 138, 2, 10: 'quid est autem civitas nisi multitudo hominum in quoddam vinculum redacta concordiae?'; also quoting Cicero; *cf.* 155, 3, 9

9 *Civ. Dei* XV, 8: 'quia nec constitui tunc ab uno poterat civitas quae nihil est aliud quam hominum multitudo aliquo societatis vinculo conligata'

10 *Civ. Dei* XIV, 28

11 See, briefly, Marshall, *Studies*, 32ff

12 *Civ. Dei* II, 21

13 *Civ. Dei* XIX, 21

14 Cicero, *De Finibus* V, 65

15 *Civ. Dei* XIX, 24; *cf.* R. T. Marshall, *Studies*, 53f

16 *Cf. Civ. Dei* II, 19; 21; R. T. Marshall, *Studies*, 80f

17 Roman disasters before Christ occupy *Civ. Dei* I–IV; the attack on the pagan gods VI–X

18 *E.g. Civ. Dei* V, 11; X, passim

19 *E.g. Civ. Dei.* IV, 28; V, 12

20 *Civ. Dei* V, 12; 21; 22

21 *Civ. Dei* V, 12

22 *Civ. Dei* V, 13 quoting Cicero, *De Republica* V, 7, 9, and, just below, *Tusc. Disp.* I, 2, 4

23 *Civ. Dei* V, 14 quoting John 5, 44

24 *Civ. Dei* V, 15

25 *Civ. Dei* V, 18

26 *Civ. Dei* V, 16

27 *Civ. Dei* V, 19; *cf.* XIX, 25

28 *Civ. Dei* IV, 21: 'ars quippe ipsa bene recteque vivendi virtus a veteribus definata est'

29 *E.g. Civ. Dei* VIII–IX; *cf.* II, 14 on Plato

30 *E.g. Civ. Dei* XIX, 4, on the four cardinal *virtutes.* One piece of pagan political philosophy Augustine could not convert or assimilate, namely the cyclic theory of history. Christian theology demanded a linear concept of historical development to the end of the world

31 *Civ. Dei* IV, 21; XXII, 24

32 *E.g. Civ. Dei* V, 14

33 *Cf. Civ. Dei* V, 14 *ad fin.*

34 *Civ. Dei* V, 14

35 *Civ. Dei* XXII, 30. Note the repeated 'political' phraseology with *gloria, honor, ambire, praemium virtutis* and especially the penultimate sentence of the quotation in the text: 'pro meritis praemiorum etiam gradus honorum atque gloriarum'

BIBLIOGRAPHY

A complete bibliography of the subject would be impossibly large. The following in the main merely records the works referred to in the notes.

AFZELIUS, A., Zur Definition der römischen Nobilität vor der Zeit Ciceros, *Class. et Med.* 1945

ALLEN, W. Caesar's *Regnum*, *T.A.P.A.*, 84, 1953

ASTIN, A. E., Scipio Aemilianus and Cato Censorius, *Latomus*, 15, 1956

BADIAN, E. *Foreign Clientelae (264–70 B.C.)*, Oxford, 1958

— *Studies in Greek and Roman History*, Oxford, 1964

— Marius and the Nobiles, *Durham University Journal*, 1964

BARDON, H., *La Littérature latine inconnue*, I, Paris, 1952

BAYNES, N. H., *The Political Ideas of St. Augustine's De Civitate Dei*, Historical Association Pamphlet No. 104, London, 1936

BIKERMAN, E., La Lettre de Mithridate dans les Histoires de Salluste, *R.E.L.* 24, 1946

BILZ, K., *Die Politik des P. Cornelius Scipio Aemilianus*, Stuttgart, 1935

BRINK, C. O. and F. W. WALBANK, The Construction of the Sixth Book of Polybius, *C.Q.* 45, 1954

CAPELLE, W., Grieschische Ethik und römischer Imperialismus, *Klio* 25, 1932

CARNEY, T. F., A Biography of C. Marius, *P.A.C.A.* Suppl. 1

COMBÈS, G., *La Doctrine politique de Saint Augustin*, Paris, 1927

CRAWFORD, O. C., Laudatio Funebris, *C.J.* 37, 1941

DOREY, T. A. (ed.) *Latin Historians*, London, 1966

— Agricola and Domitian, *Greece and Rome*, 2nd series, 7, 1960

EARL, D. C., *The Political Thought of Sallust*, Cambridge, 1961

— *Tiberius Gracchus: A Study in Politics*, Brussels, Collection Latomus LXVI, 1963

— M. Octavius trib. pleb. 133 BC and his Successor, *Latomus*, 19, 1960

EARL, D. C., Calpurnii Pisones in the Second Century BC, *Athenaeum*, 38, 1960
— Political Terminology in Plautus, *Historia*, 9, 1960
— Terence and Roman Politics, *Historia*, 11, 1962
— Sallust and the Senate's Numidian Policy, *Latomus* 24, 1965
— Review of R. Syme, Sallust, *J.R.S.* 55, 1965
— The Early Career of Sallust, *Historia*, 15, 1966
ECKSTADT, K., *Augustins Anschauung vom Staat*, Kirchain, 1912
ENSSLIN, W., Zur Geschichtschreibung und Weltanschauung des Ammianus Marcellinus, *Klio* XVI, 1923
ERNOUT, A., Les Noms Latins en –TUS, *Philologica Classica*, Paris, 1946
ERNOUT A. and A. MEILLET, *Dictionnaire Etymologique de la Langue Latine*, Paris, 3rd. ed., 1951
FIGGIS, J. N., *The Political Aspects of St. Augustine's City of God*, London, 1921
FRAENKEL, E., *Horace*, Oxford, 1957
FRANK, TENNEY, The Scipionic Inscriptions, *C.Q.* 15, 1921
FRIBERG, H. F., *Love and Justice in Political Theory, A Study of Augustine's Definition of the Commonwealth*, Chicago, 1944
VON FRITZ, K., Tacitus, Agricola, Domitian and the Problem of the Principate, *C.Ph.* 52, 1957
FUCHS, H., *Augustin und der antike Friedensgedanke*, Berlin, 1926
GABBA, E., Studi su Dionigi da Alicarnasso, *Athenaeum*, 38, 1960
GELZER, M., *Die Nobilität der Römischen Republik*, Berlin, 1912
— *Vom römischen Staat*, I, Leipzig, 1943
— Nasicas Widerspruch gegen die Zerstörung Karthagos, *Phil.* 86, 1931
GIBBON, EDWARD, *The Decline and Fall of the Roman Empire*, ed. J. B. Bury, London, 1900–14
GIMAZANE, J., *Ammien Marcellin: sa vie et son œuvre*, Toulouse, 1889
HELLEGOUARC'H, J., *Le Vocabulaire Latin des Relations et des Partis Politiques sous la République*, Paris, 1963
HILL, H., *The Roman Middle Class*, Oxford, 1952
HOCH, H., *Die Darstellung der politische Sendung Roms*, Frankfurt am Main, 1951
JONES, A. H. M., *Studies in Roman Government and Law*, Oxford, 1960
— *The Later Roman Empire 284–602*, Oxford, 1964
KEINAST, D., *Cato der Zensor*, Heidelberg, 1954
LAMBRECHTS, P., *La Composition du sénat romain de l'accession au trône d'Hadrien à la mort de Commode*, Anvers and Paris, 1936

LEPORE, E., *Il Princeps Ciceroniano e gli ideali politichi della tarda Repubblica*, Naples, 1954
MARROU, H. I. *Saint Augustin et la fin de la culture antique*, Paris, 1938
— *Saint Augustin et la fin de la culture antique, Retractatio*, Paris, 1949
MARSHALL, R. T., *Studies in the Political and Socio-Religious Terminology of the De Civitate Dei*, Catholic University of America, Patristic Studies LXXXVI, Washington D.C., 1952
MCDONALD, A. H., Rome and the Italian Confederation (200–186 BC), *J.R.S.* 34, 1944
MOMMSEN, T., *Römische Forschungen*, Berlin, 1864, 1879
— *Römisches Staatsrecht*, Leipzig, 3rd ed., 1887–9
OFFERGELT, F., *Die Staatslehre des hlg. Augustinus nach seinen samtlichen Werken*, Bonn, 1914
OGILVIE, R. M., *A Commentary on Livy Books 1–5*, Oxford, 1965
PÖSCHL, V., *The Art of Virgil*, Ann Arbor, 1962
VAN OMME, A. N., *Virtus, een semantiese studie*, Diss. Utrecht, n.d.
ROLOFF, H., *Maiores bei Cicero*, Gottingen, 1938
ROWELL, HENRY T., *Ammianus Marcellinus, Soldier-Historian of the Late Roman Empire*, University of Cincinnati, 1964
DE SANCTIS, G., *Storia dei Romani* I–IV, i, Turin. 1907–23; IV, ii, Florence, 1953–8
SCHILLING, O., *Die Staats- und Soziallehre des hl. Augustinus*, Freiburg im Breisgau, 1910
SCHMEKEL, A., *Die Philosophie der mittleren Stoa*, Berlin, 1892
SCULLARD, H. H., *Roman Politics 220–150 B.C.*, Oxford, 1951
SHERWIN-WHITE, A. N., *The Roman Citizenship*, Oxford, 1939
— Violence in Roman Politics, *J.R.S.* 46, 1956
SIMON, H., *Roms Krieg in Spanien, 154–133 v. Chr.*, Frankfurt, 1962
SMITH, R. E., *The Aristocratic Epoch in Latin Literature*, Sydney, 1947
STRASBURGER, H., Poseidonius on the Problems of the Roman Empire, *J.R.S.* 55, 1965
SUERBAUM, W., *Vom antiken zum frühmittelalterlichen Staatsbegriff*, Munster, 1961
SYME, R., *The Roman Revolution*, Oxford, 1939
— *Tacitus*, Oxford, 1958
— *Sallust*, Berkeley and Los Angeles, Cambridge, 1964
— Caesar, the Senate and Italy, *P.B.S.R.* 14, 1938
— Marcus Lepidus, *Capax Imperii*, *J.R.S.* 45, *1955*
— Livy and Augustus, *Harvard Studies in Classical Philology*, 64, 1959
TAYLOR, L. R., *Party Politics in the Age of Caesar*, Berkeley, 1949

TAYLOR, L. R., The Forerunners of the Gracchi, *J.R.S.* 52, 1962

THOMPSON, E. A., *The Historical Work of Ammianus Marcellinus*, Cambridge, 1947

TRAUB, H. W., Agricola's Refusal of a Governorship, *C.Ph.* 49, 1954

TREU, M., Zur Clementia Caesars, *Museum Helveticum*, 5, 1948

VOGT, J., *Homo novus, ein Typus der römischen Republik*, Stuttgart, 1926

— *Ammianus Marcellinus als erzählender Geschichtsschreiber der Spätzeit*, Mainz, 1963

WALBANK, F. W., Political Morality and the Friends of Scipio, *J.R.S.* 55, 1965

WALSH, P., *Livy, His Historical Aims and Methods*, Cambridge, 1961

WEGEHAUPT, H., *Die Bedeutung und Anwendung von Dignitas in der Schriften der republikanischen Zeit*, Diss. Breslau, 1932

WILLEMS, P., *Le Sénat de la République romaine*, Louvain, 1878–83

WIRSZUBSKI, C., *Libertas as a Political Idea at Rome during the Late Republic and Early Principate*, Cambridge, 1950

INDEX

Proper names are entered under *nomina* with the exception of the names of emperors and members of the imperial family.